CAMPAIGN • 244

THE FALKLANDS 1982

Ground operations in the South Atlantic

G FREMONT-BARNES　　　ILLUSTRATED BY G TURNER

Series editor Marcus Cowper

First published in Great Britain in 2012 by Osprey Publishing,
Midland House, West Way, Botley, Oxford OX2 0PH, UK
44-02 23rd St, Suite 219, Long Island City, NY 11101, USA

E-mail: info@ospreypublishing.com

© 2012 Osprey Publishing Ltd

A CIP catalogue record for this book is available from the British Library.

ISBN: 978 1 84908 607 3
PDF e-book ISBN: 978 1 84908 608 0
EPUB e-book ISBN: 978 1 78096 416 4

Editorial by Ilios Publishing Ltd, Oxford, UK (www.iliospublishing.com)
Page layout by: The Black Spot
Index by Sandra Shotter
Typeset in Sabon and Myriad Pro
Maps by Bounford.com
3D bird's-eye view by The Black Spot
Battlescene illustrations by Graham Turner
Originated by Blenheim Colour Ltd
Printed in China through Worldprint

12 13 14 15 16   10 9 8 7 6 5 4 3 2 1

DEDICATION

This book is dedicated to my younger son, Monty, who like the Paras and
Marines holds a special appreciation for the merits of physical fitness.

ARTIST'S NOTE

Readers may care to note that the original paintings from which the
color plates in this book were prepared are available for private sale.
The Publishers retain all reproduction copyright whatsoever.
All enquiries should be addressed to:

Graham Turner, PO Box 568, Aylesbury, Bucks, HP17 8EX, UK
www.studio88.co.uk

The Publishers regret that they can enter into no correspondence
upon this matter.

THE WOODLAND TRUST

Osprey Publishing are supporting the Woodland Trust, the UK's leading
woodland conservation charity, by funding the dedication of trees.

IMPERIAL WAR MUSEUM COLLECTIONS

Many of the photos in this book come from the Imperial War Museum's
huge collections which cover all aspects of conflict involving Britain and
the Commonwealth since the start of the twentieth century.

These rich resources are available online to search, browse and buy at
www.iwmcollections.org.uk. In addition to Collections Online, you can
visit the Visitors Rooms where you can explore over 8 million photgraphs,
thousands of hours of moving images, the largest sound archive of its
kind in the world, thousands of diaries and letters written by people
in wartime, and a huge reference library. To make an appointment call
(020) 7416 5320, or email mail@iwm.org.uk. Imperial War Museum
www.iwm.org.uk.

Key to military symbols

Army Group	Army	Corps	Division	Brigade	Regiment	Battalion
Company/Battery	Platoon	Section	Squad	Infantry	Artillery	Cavalry
Airborne	Unit HQ	Air defence	Air Force	Air mobile	Air transportable	Amphibious
Anti-tank	Armour	Air aviation	Bridging	Engineer	Headquarters	Maintenance
Medical	Missile	Mountain	Navy	Nuclear, biological, chemical	Ordnance	Parachute
Reconnaissance	Signal	Supply	Transport movement	Rocket artillery	Air defence artillery	

Key to unit identification

Unit identifier / Parent unit / Commander / (+) with added elements / (−) less elements

CONTENTS

Theatre of operations, April–June 1982

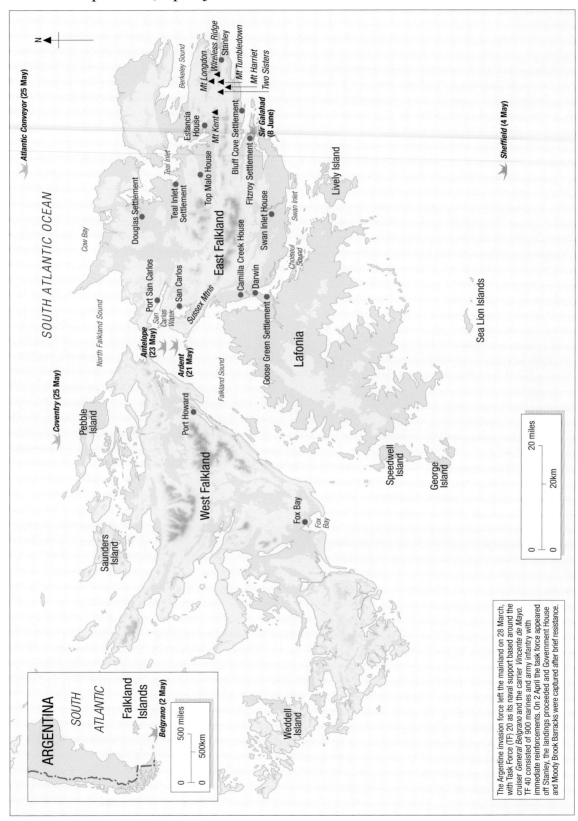

N

Atlantic Conveyor (25 May)

Berkeley Sound

Wireless Ridge
Stanley
Mt Longdon
Mt Tumbledown
Mt Harriet
Two Sisters

Estancia House

Mt Kent ▲

Bluff Cove Settlement

Sir Galahad (8 June)

SOUTH ATLANTIC OCEAN

Teal Inlet

Top Malo House

Teal Inlet Settlement

Fitzroy Settlement

Lively Island

Douglas Settlement

Cow Bay

Swan Inlet House

Swan Inlet

Sheffield (4 May)

East Falkland

Choiseul Sound

Coventry (25 May)

North Falkland Sound

Port San Carlos

San Carlos Water

San Carlos

Sussex Mtns

Antelope (23 May)

Ardent (21 May)

Camilla Creek House

Darwin

Goose Green Settlement

Sea Lion Islands

Lafonia

Falkland Sound

Pebble Island

Port Howard

Speedwell Island

George Island

West Falkland

Fox Bay

Fox Bay

Saunders Island

Weddell Island

20 miles

0

20km

0

ARGENTINA

SOUTH ATLANTIC

Falkland Islands

Belgrano (2 May)

500 miles

0

500km

0

The Argentine invasion force left the mainland on 28 March, with Task Force (TF) 20 as its naval support based around the cruiser *General Belgrano* and the carrier *Vincente de Mayo*. TF 40 consisted of 900 marines and army infantry with immediate reinforcements. On 2 April the task force appeared off Stanley, the landings proceeded and Government House and Moody Brook Barracks were captured after brief resistance.

INTRODUCTION

No history of the Falklands campaign is complete without viewing the war in the context of all its phases and all the arms of service involved. Thus, while this volume concentrates on ground operations, an effort has been made to set it in context of the air and naval operations. Yet, at the end of the day, some of the most dramatic episodes must be seen as preliminary stages in the ultimate phase of the campaign: operations on land, particularly in the aftermath of Goose Green. Thus, Admiral Woodward's naval operations, the sinking of the *Belgrano*, the loss of the *Sheffield*, the operations conducted by Argentine Super Etendards and British Harriers, the attack on the *Sir Galahad* – all are here subordinated to the operations of ground forces, from the landings at San Carlos, through the initial attack at Goose Green to the final push through the mountains west of Stanley.

The war is remarkable on many counts: the long period of build-up by the British and the slow and steady approach of the Task Force, which represented gradual, mounting pressure by an expeditionary force operating at the extreme limits of its abilities. It represents a classic conventional conflict – a rare feature indeed of modern warfare – with no atrocities committed against civilians, no guerrilla operations as an adjunct to the principal operations, and relatively low casualties – with about 250 British and over

LEFT
The most iconic image of the ground campaign: 45 Commando Royal Marines approaches Stanley in single file down a rough track. (Imperial War Museum, FKD 2028)

RIGHT
Royal Marines raising the Union Jack on landing at San Carlos on 21 May. Land operations concluded in little more than three weeks – with time of the essence in light of deteriorating weather conditions which affected operations in the air, at sea as well as on the ground. (Imperial War Museum, FKD 77)

A jubilant Argentine marine of the Amphibious Vehicles Battalion on top of his vehicle after the occupation of Stanley. Approximately 900 troops comprised the invasion force. (Imperial War Museum, FKD 2166)

1,000 Argentines killed. The initial phase of the war necessarily focused on the build-up for Operation *Corporate*, which set in motion a rapid mobilization of British air, land and sea forces. Specifically, ships and aircraft were prepared hastily for the transport of a force of Marines, Paras and other Army units

The final offensive in June represented the greatest effort by the British Army since World War II – though on nothing like the scale of operations of that conflict – with the equivalent of a mere seven battalions, with artillery and limited air and armour in support. Still, the campaign represented a Herculean task on the part of the logistic and support services, with supply lines stretched 8,000 miles (13,000km) back to Britain. For the Argentines, their forces operated much closer to home – a mere 400 miles (650km) – yet circumstances posed a number of unforeseen complications: bleak conditions for those deployed outside Stanley, irregular supplies of food, inadequate protection from the weather, and an uncertainty about where the blow would fall if and when the British managed to acquire a foothold in the islands. Both sides suffered privations in very cold, often extremely wet, conditions, with biting cold, sleet, snow and Antarctic winds adding to the complications imposed on the British attempt to take ground against troops superior in number, well dug-in and possessing excellent fields of fire. From the fall of South Georgia through the fatally exposed ground at Goose Green to the formidable, rocky face of Mt Tumbledown, the two ground forces contested one of the world's most remote and inhospitable places in the defence of their declared sovereign rights – all conducted in one of the fastest-moving major conflicts of modern times. The ground operations of the Falklands War reveal basic operational lessons often ignored, however often in the past the same principles had proven themselves timeless: that the advantages bestowed by superior numbers – even when holding a defensive position and blessed with greater firepower – count for comparatively little when faced with highly professional, well-led, superbly trained, exceptionally fit troops imbued with a strong sense of purpose and enjoying high morale.

The Argentines wallowed under the misconception that technology and force of numbers could prevail against determined professionals. They lacked the essentials of training, discipline and skill at arms – features prominent in the units of their opponents – relying instead on holding (albeit sometimes impressive) fixed positions and thus abandoning the initiative to the British. Superior firepower and, in some instances, better equipment, ought to have stood the Argentines in better stead; but so woeful were their tactics of static defence, combined with the failure even to launch unplanned counterattacks, much less well-planned and coordinated efforts, and so low had sunk their level of motivation after the initial euphoria of their occupation of the islands, that any prospect of success on the ground withered as the British moved from success to success, emboldened as they went, even when faced with exhausting marches and freezing conditions. Let there be no mistake: the British were not 'supermen' but faced an enemy unwilling – but by no means unable – to make a determined stand against them. The outcome seemed all but inevitable so long as British forces could maintain the momentum of attack, which, in the event, they did.

Memorial to the fallen of Mt Tumbledown, one of the five rocky outcrops just west of Stanley which witnessed fighting during the British offensive to repossess the Falkland Islands. (UK MOD/Crown Copyright 2012)

CHRONOLOGY

19 March	Scrap metal merchants land at disused whaling station at Leith on South Georgia and raise Argentine flag.
21 March	HMS *Endurance* embarks with Royal Marine (RM) detachment and part of Naval Party (NP) 8901 and sails for South Georgia.
22 March	*Bahía Buen Suceso* departs from Leith Harbour, leaving behind several dozen scrap metal workers.
24 March	*Endurance* lands RM contingent to monitor Argentine activities at Leith.
25 March	*Bahía Paraíso* lands Argentine marines at Leith.
29 March	New NP 8901 arrives at Stanley. Junta approves final plan for invasion.
31 March	*Endurance* disembarks her RM detachment at Grytviken, South Georgia.
1 April	RM garrison on Falklands deploy to defensive positions around Stanley.
2 April	Argentine troops invade Falklands. Governor Hunt orders NP 8901 to surrender after it offers spirited resistance. Task Force prepares for deployment; 3 Commando Brigade readied.
3 April	Argentines defeat small contingent of RM at Grytviken.
5 April	Task Force sails from Plymouth with HQ 3 Commando Brigade and elements of 40 and 42 Commandos.
11 April	M Coy Gp of 42 Commando embark HMS *Antrim* at Ascension Island and sails.
12 April	Britain declares 200-mile (320km) Maritime Exclusion Zone (MEZ) around the Falklands.

16 April	Task Force sails from Ascension.
21 April	Wessex from *Antrim* recces and drops SBS and SAS on South Georgia.
22 April	SAS evacuated from Fortuna Glacier; two Wessex helicopters crash.
23 April	M Coy 42 Commando land on South Georgia.
26 April	Lt. Cdr. Astiz surrenders on South Georgia.
28 April	Britain announces Total Exclusion Zone (TEZ) to include aircraft and ships of all nations.
30 April	Britain enforces 200-mile (320km) TEZ; main Task Force reaches TEZ.
1 May	Maj. Gen. Moore appointed land deputy to C-in-C Fleet; RMS *Queen Elizabeth II* requisitioned.
2 May	Submarine HMS *Conqueror* sinks *General Belgrano*.
4 May	*Sheffield* hit by Exocet missile; she sinks six days later.
6 May	2 Para arrives at Ascension.
7 May	Main body of Amphibious Task Group leaves Ascension.
12 May	*QE 2* sails from Southampton with 5 Infantry Brigade; operation order for landings issued to 3 Commando Brigade.
14 May	SAS raid Pebble Island, destroying all Argentine aircraft present.
21 May	Amphibious landings made by 3 Commando Brigade at San Carlos. HMS *Ardent* sunk.
22 May	3 Commando Brigade established ashore at Ajax Bay.
22–27 May	Sustained succession of intense Argentine air attacks against vessels at the beachhead.
23 May	HMS *Antelope* sunk.
25 May	HMS *Coventry* and transport vessel *Atlantic Conveyor* sunk by Exocet missiles.
26 May	2 Para starts advance on Goose Green.
27 May	45 Commando and 3 Para commence 'yomp' and 'tab' from San Carlos; SAS patrol flown to Mount Kent; 5 Infantry Brigade begins cross decking.

28 May	Battle of Goose Green.
29 May	Argentines surrender at Goose Green; over 900 prisoners taken.
30 May	Maj. Gen. Moore arrives in the Falklands and replaces Thompson as commander of land operations; Thompson resumes as commander of 3 Commando Brigade.
31 May	42 Commando moves by air to Mount Kent; Mountain and Arctic Warfare Cadre attacks Argentine Special Forces at Top Malo House; 45 Commando reaches Teal Inlet; 3 Para reaches Douglas Settlement.
1 June	5 Infantry Brigade begins disembarking at San Carlos; 3 Commando Brigade forward HQ established at Teal Inlet; 42 and 45 Commandos and 3 Para begin regular, intensive patrolling of mountains west of Stanley.
2 June	2 Para flown to Bluff Cove.
5 June	Scots Guards embark for Fitzroy in *Sir Tristram*.
6 June	Welsh Guards embark for Fitzroy in HMS *Fearless* but ship withheld.
	Scots Guards land at Fitzroy, where 5 Infantry Brigade establishes forward base.
8 June	Argentine aircraft bomb *Sir Galahad* and *Sir Tristram* at Fitzroy, killing dozens of Welsh Guardsmen; Moore finalizes plans for final offensive.
11–12 June	3 Para attacks Mount Longdon; 42 Commando attacks Mount Harriet; 45 Commando attacks Two Sisters.
13–14 June	2 Para attacks Wireless Ridge; Scots Guards attacks Tumbledown; 1/7 Gurkhas occupies Mt William.
14 June	Brig. Gen. Menéndez surrenders all Argentine forces in the Falklands.

OPPOSING COMMANDERS

ARGENTINE COMMANDERS

Very little is known of the character and background of Argentine senior commanders in the Falklands.

Fifty-two-year-old **Brigadier-General Mario Menéndez** was appointed Governor and Commander-in-Chief Malvinas (the Argentine name for the Falklands). After the war he recalled the circumstances of his appointment:

> I first realised I was going to be involved in a Malvinas operation in the first week of March of 1982 during a meeting with General Galtieri [the president]. I was Major General of the Army, an important position. When I had completed making my report and we were alone, General Galtieri said to me, 'Now I have to say something.' He then told me that the Argentine government, or rather the military junta, were considering taking military action in the Malvinas if they did not achieve any headway in the conversations they were having with the English, in particular with regard to sovereignty. General Galtieri told me that depending on how things developed, there would be military action, and I would be designated Military Governor: 'Start to revise your English, and prepare yourself to see what you can do in the Malvinas.'

Brigadier-General Oscar Luis Joffre initially commanded 10th Brigade, in the Stanley area, a formation with a good standard of equipment, including armoured personnel carriers and a squadron of armoured cars. Later he led all units in the Stanley sector. Joffre was a man of large stature and known by the nickname 'the horse', owing to his imposing size and the shape of his face. He held the respect of his men – a characteristic not universal in an army known at times for the sharp divisions between officers and other ranks – possessed remarkable energy and exchanged many heated communications with unit commanders during the battles in the mountains around Stanley. **Brigadier-General Parada** commanded the remainder of the islands, including the western part of East Falkland and the whole of West Falkland.

The early planning for the invasion was largely undertaken by **Rear Admiral Carlos Büsser**, the Commander of Marines and an enthusiastic supporter of operations to occupy the Falklands and South Georgia. He established a five-man committee in Puerto Belgrano to study the requirements of an amphibious landing, recounting it in outline thus: 'My overall plan was to capture Government House and the Royal Marines' barracks at Moody

Brook by surprise and, if possible, without bloodshed. To do this I decided to come in from many directions and with a crushing superiority. I hoped for a psychological effect that would be overwhelming.'

BRITISH COMMANDERS

As the retaking of the Falkland Islands centred around maritime operations, the Royal Navy figured more prominently than the Army (and the Royal Air Force), with Admiral Sir John Fieldhouse, the Commander-in-Chief Fleet, appointed the Task Force Commander, his headquarters based in Northwood in Middlesex, near London. There a large staff coordinated all air, sea and land operations; however, as this volume focuses on ground operations, it is appropriate to concentrate on those commanders most associated with that aspect of the campaign.

Once it was decided that 3 Commando Brigade would serve as the first of the ground forces deployed in theatre, it was logical that the Chief Military Adviser should be drawn from the Royal Marines. This position therefore naturally fell to **Major-General Jeremy Moore** who, though intending to retire in May, remained in post as the senior Royal Marines General Officer as a result of the serious injury sustained by the Commandant General of the Royal Marines at the hands of an IRA bomb in December 1981. Moore and his staff shifted their HQ from Portsmouth to Northwood, serving initially as an adviser in the role of Land Forces Deputy and later, on 20 May, appointed field commander as Commander Land Forces Falkland Islands. His divisional rank, his and his staff's close understanding of combined operations and the fact that he had been involved from the beginning in an advisory capacity, made him a sound choice, notwithstanding the fact that of the eight battalions involved, five would be drawn from the Army. Moore left Britain for Ascension on 16 April for a planning meeting with Commodore Clapp, commander of the Amphibious Task Group, Brig. Thompson and Admiral

Brigadier Julian Thompson (centre) and Major-General Jeremy Moore (right), commander of 3 Commando Brigade and Commander Land Forces, Falkland Islands, respectively. (Royal Marines Museum)

Senior commanders of the Argentine invasion force tour Port Stanley on 2 April. Left to right: unknown air force officer, Lieutenant-General Osvaldo Garcia (overall commander of the Argentine invasion force), Rear Admiral Carlos Büsser (commander of the Argentine Marines force) and Rear Admiral Gualater Allara (commander of Task Force 40, which provided naval support for the landings). (Imperial War Museum, FKD 2169)

Woodward. Throughout the conflict Moore showed himself a capable commander, regularly visited his units, encouraged his men and always maintained his nerve when circumstances might have weakened those of a lesser commander overwhelmed by the formidable task at hand.

Of the initial five task group commanders, all of whom reported directly to the Task Force Commander, Rear Admiral 'Sandy' Woodward commanded the Carrier Battle Task Group; Commodore Mike Clapp led the Amphibious Task Group; Vice Admiral Peter Herbert commanded the Submarine Task Group; and Captain Brian Young led the South Georgia Group. Finally, and most relevant here, was **Brigadier Julian Thompson**, commander of the Landing Force Group. Thompson had been commander of 3 Commando Brigade since January 1981, having completed service in 40 and 42 Commandos in the Middle East, with 45 Commando in Aden, and 43 Commando in Britain. He returned to 40 Commando in the Far East, was promoted to Brigade Major of 3 Commando Brigade and later led 40 Commando during his tour in Ulster. Thereafter he served on the staff of Headquarters Commando Forces. Once Moore was appointed commander of land forces on 20 May, Thompson continued briefly in his existing capacity since Moore was still at sea aboard the *QE2*, then serving as a troopship, and had no direct communications with the amphibious force. When Moore's divisional headquarters arrived on 30 May, however, Moore formally assumed command of Land Forces Falkland Islands, while Thompson reverted to commanding 3 Commando Brigade. Thompson bore the burden of the subsequent land operations extremely well, and much of the success of those operations must be attributed to his leadership and careful planning.

Brigadier Tony Wilson, a 47-year-old light infantryman, commanded the reserve force of 5 Infantry Brigade, which left Britain after 3 Commando Brigade and consisted of 1st Battalion The Welsh Guards, 2nd Battalion The Scots Guards and 1st Battalion The 7th Gurkhas. Wilson had won the Military Cross and OBE in Northern Ireland. He would lead the advance on Stanley from the south, but his decision to shift his units without proper support, particularly the Welsh Guards, would lead him into disfavour after the war.

OPPOSING FORCES

ARGENTINE GROUND FORCES

Argentina's army (Ejército), numbering approximately 60,000 troops, compared favourably with other South American forces, though most of its troops consisted of conscripts serving a year in the ranks and consequently varied in quality. The brigade functioned as the principal operational unit, with each performing a specialized function according to its type: armoured, mechanized, infantry, mountain, jungle and airmobile. Each brigade comprised three infantry battalions plus one artillery and one engineer battalion. The Army also had five anti-aircraft battalions and one aviation battalion. Army and marine units on the Falklands had at their disposal Panhard armoured cars, 105mm and 155mm artillery, 20mm, 30mm and 35mm anti-aircraft guns, and Roland, Tigercat and Blowpipe surface-to-air missiles (SAMs). A branch of the Navy, the Marine Corps (Infanteria de Marina) consisted of 6,000 personnel composing two Fleet Marine forces, each of which contained two infantry battalions and support troops. The assault commandos, or Buzos Tácticos, supplied part of the landing force, together with approximately 800 men from the 2nd Marine Infantry Battalion. A second battalion was later deployed near Stanley.

Wearing padded parkas, US Army issue steel helmets, olive drab fatigues and high black combat boots, the typical Argentine soldier carried equipment harness (in British parlance, 'webbing') usually of grey-green leather, bayonets frogged on the left hip, a canteen, and a small pack on the right hip. Leather gloves were used extensively, together with field caps with pile-lined flaps. In addition, they carried the light 'assault packs', to which they attached a blanket and a spade thrust under the straps at the back. Alternatively, soldiers carried horseshoe blankets rolled around their bodies. Weapons included the heavy-barrel light machine gun, the US 3.5in. rocket launcher fitted with a folding bipod, and as many as six rifle grenades attached to the front and sides of a vest. Marine commandos carried the Sterling 9mm machine gun. Argentine ration packs came in two varieties: the standard type issued to the rank and file and, for officers, a larger pack containing a greater portion and a higher quality of food, as well as cigarettes and whisky. This inequitable system almost certainly contributed to the alienation many soldiers experienced from their officers.

A mythology has grown around the campaign with respect to differentiating the performance of units containing professional troops and those composed solely of conscripts. In truth, with the exception of some elite formations, all units contained a mixture of both, consistent with other national armies operating a system of national service. Thus, newly inducted conscripts populated all units together with a cadre of professional soldiers, NCOs and officers. Normally an infantry unit contained an average of 25 per cent new recruits, but some units, owing to the rapid need to increase their strength through cross-posting from other regiments, contained a greater proportion of men with relatively little military experience.

Argentine forces based in Stanley itself mostly served in administrative, headquarters or support units and generally lived well, enjoying decent though by no means lavish accommodation, shower facilities and hot food. Living amongst the civilian population, moreover, they remained virtually immune from air and artillery attack. Those units deployed on the coast around Stanley and at the airport, together with artillery and air force personnel, had less access to 'creature comforts', although they could occasionally visit the town and did not suffer from severe weather conditions like their comrades deployed in the hills. These troops experienced considerable discomfort and sometimes misery in their exposed positions on high ground. Although situated no further than 7 miles (11km) from Stanley, they possessed no transport and seldom, if ever, visited the town. Such troops had already been *in situ* well before the arrival of the Task Force, so condemning them to over six weeks in the mountains – twice the time spent by British troops in the open. Worse still, the principal burden of the coming British offensive would fall upon the shoulders of these hungry, cold and debilitated troops.

Specifically, these men lived miserably in tents, trenches or shelters improvised from stones and turf, faced intense cold and wind, and endured hunger and fatigue as a remorseless experience. Digging in proved extremely difficult owing to the thin layer of soil through which water rapidly penetrated and beneath which a lower layer absorbed and retained the water. Trenches consequently became waterlogged or even flooded when it rained. Frostbite and 'trench foot' were common maladies, leading to continuous loss of personnel through sickness. Even troops entitled to walk to Stanley on a weekly basis in search of small comforts often declined to make the trek owing to extreme hunger and weakness. As one conscript from the 7th Regiment on Mt Longdon explained:

We were cold, wet and hungry – really very hungry – and tired. Our equipment was good, but we really didn't get the material to keep it clean; things got very rusty. There was no possibility of washing your clothes – and certainly none of getting them dry afterwards. I had three issue pants and three of my own; I just threw most of them away in the end. I had three pairs of socks; I wore them all at once and never changed them. Our clothes had been the ones issued in La Plata – for the climate of La Plata [i.e., balmy].... We had three thin blankets, a sleeping-bag and a thin mattress each – not enough to keep us warm, but we would lie together with another man and share.

The shortage of food became acute and affected morale severely. Tea was available, but no milk and only small quantities of sugar. Troops often had to suffice with a thin soup, made of dehydrated vegetables and very little meat for both lunch and dinner. Bread, a basic Argentine staple, was nowhere to be found, though sheep, available in abundance, could be shot and slaughtered. Some men situated outside Stanley resorted to trying to steal from the store at Moody Brook, since what the army issued for a week's supply many soldiers devoured within a day or two, with another five days' wait before the commissariat issued the next ration pack.

Even then, troops stationed outside Stanley regularly found their rations and gift packages sent from home looted, presumably by those in the logistic corps or operating the postal service in the town. Cigarettes tended to be plentiful, but even these might be purloined by those with access to the mountains of supplies based in Stanley, selling them on for profit. Even where supplies stood in abundance, conveying them out of Stanley posed major challenges owing to a severe lack of adequate transport given the often trackless and universally rough nature of the ground. Even shifting essentials like ammunition often required men to serve as beasts of burden, leaving them exhausted by the effort. To compound these already formidable problems, some units' cooking equipment had been left behind in Argentina, denying large numbers of men regular hot meals – a factor not as critical in terms of nutrition as for the maintenance of morale in circumstances that required a high calorific intake. Soldiers drawn from the slums of Buenos Aires tended to cope much better than those accustomed to relatively comfortable lives, but the strain from boredom, fatigue, cold and hunger became palpable across all units; hope of evacuation home led a few soldiers to self-inflict wounds.

Many troops endured unnecessary privation owing to inadequate clothing. The 5th Marines, for instance, normally posted to Tierra del Fuego in the extreme south of mainland Argentina, numbered amongst the only troops of the three units occupying the mountains west of Stanley kitted out with proper cold-weather clothing, and specifically trained to cope in the severe conditions encountered on the Falklands. By marked contrast, the 4th Regiment – deployed on Mt Harriet and Two Sisters – was not acclimatized as their recruitment and training area was situated in a subtropical region of Argentina.

Food supply improved just prior to the British advance, as did the situation of the wounded, who were regularly evacuated to the mainland, but even when food quantities proved adequate, the distribution system functioned so poorly that forward units experienced great difficulty receiving fresh and cooked food. The bone-chilling cold only exacerbated the need for high-calorific sustenance and yet the paradox remained: tons of food sat at Stanley waterfront but no means existed to move it to outlying areas despite the short distances to the mountains, leaving a sharp disparity between the health and morale of troops living in the open and those established in relative comfort in the capital.

BRITISH GROUND FORCES

Ground forces prominent in the recapture of the Falklands included 40, 42, and 45 Commandos, Royal Marines, the first two based near Plymouth and the last at Arbroath in Scotland; 2nd and 3rd Battalions The Parachute Regiment (2 and 3 Para), based at Aldershot; 1st Battalion The 7th Royal Gurkha Rifles (1/7 Gurkhas) based at Church Crookham; finally, 2nd Battalion The Scots Guards (2 Scots Guards) and 1st Battalion The Welsh Guards (1 Welsh Guards) based at Wellington Barracks in London. These units ranked amongst the best of Britain's armed forces; put simply, the British soldier and Marine could march faster, entrench himself more effectively and shoot more accurately than his Argentine counterpart, who enjoyed a much lower standard of marksmanship, fieldcraft and general discipline. British troops were entirely volunteers, often with many years' experience, National Service in Britain having been abolished 20 years before. This fact alone rendered UK forces innately superior to the overwhelming majority of recruits in Argentine service, and more than equal to those who composed even the professional cadre.

British infantry and Royal Marines wore camouflage of light green, yellow, light red-brown and black, with a variety of helmets or unit berets. Units in the Army wore 'Northern Ireland' boots and sometimes overboots or puttees, which were intended for use in central Europe rather than the topography and climate of the South Atlantic, while the Marines wore more sensible footwear designed for use in Arctic conditions. Equipment was standard 1958-pattern issue, together with a variety of rucksacks, a windproof suit, waterbottle, NBC (Nuclear, Biological, Chemical) gear, poncho roll and a lightweight shovel, to mention but a few items of 'kit' they carried. The self-loading rifle or SLR, served as the standard infantry weapon, with Trilux sight attached.

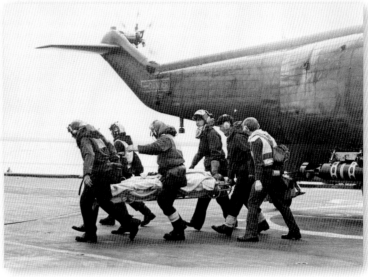

Other infantry weapons included the light machine gun – a modified 7.62mm form of the popular Bren LMG from World War II – and the much heavier .50-cal. machine gun. The Blowpipe, a surface-to-air missile, could be carried and deployed by an individual soldier, providing close-range defence against aircraft attacking at low altitude. Radio or optical tracking guided the missile which, with its high-explosive warhead, weighed 47lbs (21kg) and measured 4ft 7in. (1.5m) in length, making it a formidable load on the back of its hapless carrier. It was remarkably effective against dug-in enemy positions, but added considerably to the burden already borne by soldiers nearly always moving without the benefit of helicopter transport. An individual infantryman might also carry a Milan, a wire-guided missile fired from the shoulder, intended for use against armour but discovered in the course of the campaign to be highly effective against Argentine bunkers and sangars. Its guidance system relied simply on keeping the target in the crosshairs as the missile hurtled forward to a maximum range of 2,200 yards (2,000m). The Milan's hollow-charge high-explosive warhead could penetrate most armour plate and, as with the Blowpipe, proved devastating against the trenches at Goose Green and the defensive positions the Argentines dug or erected in the mountains west of Stanley.

The standard 81mm mortar provided further support to the infantry, firing at a rate of 15rpm and sending ordnance with considerable accuracy to distances of between 4,900 and 6,100 yards (4,500 and 5,600m) depending on the strength of the charge employed. Rounds weighed almost 10lb (5kg) each and consisted of various types suited to a specific purpose: high explosive, white phosphorus, smoke or illumination. The mortar itself weighed almost 80lb (35kg) and required a three-man team to operate it as part of the specialist mortar platoon of a battalion's support company.

ORDERS OF BATTLE

ARGENTINE GROUND FORCES IN THE FALKLANDS AND ON SOUTH GEORGIA (INITIALLY, 2,000, RISING TO 13,000 PERSONNEL)

Those units deployed in the Falklands by the time the British Task Force landed on 21 May were not in many cases the same as those which conducted the original invasion on 2 April, which at that time consisted of elements of the 2nd Fleet Marine Force. Apart from the eight vessels comprising the naval component of Task Force 40 for Operation *Blue*, the landing component under Rear Admiral Carlos Büsser totalled 904 personnel and consisted of the following:

601st Marine Commando Company
1st and 2nd Marine Infantry Battalions
Command and Services Battalion
Amphibious Reconnaissance Group
1st Amphibious Vehicles Battalion (incl. 20 Amtracs
　　and 15 x LARC-5)
Various anti-tank, heavy mortar and engineer companies
Marine Field Artillery Battalion – 6 x 105mm guns
Detachment of Buzos Tácticos

Most of these forces were replaced with the following units, whose names are translated from the Spanish, about which the data below constitutes the best available, though it may contain errors in minor details:

Army Group Malvinas
Special Forces
　　601st Commando Company
　　602nd Commando Company
　　601st Company, National Gendarmerie

Cavalry
181st Armoured Reconnaissance Squadron
Grenadier Regiment 'General San Martin'

Artillery and Air Defence
4th Airlifted Artillery Group
601st Air Defence Group
602nd Air Defence Group

Combat and Service Support
601st Combat Engineer Company
601st Combat Aviation Group
601st Combat Aviation Maintenance Group
181st Communications Company
181st Military Police Company

181st Military Intelligence Company
601st Buildings and Logistics Company

3rd Mechanized Infantry Brigade – Brig. Gen. Parada
4th Infantry Regiment
5th Infantry Regiment
12th Infantry Regiment
3rd Artillery Group
101st Artillery Group
3rd Logistics Battalion
3rd Combat Engineers Company
3rd Communication Company

9th Mechanized Infantry Brigade – Brig. Gen. Daher
8th Infantry Battalion
25th Infantry Battalion
9th Logistics Battalion
9th Combat Engineers Company
9th Communications Company
9th Medical Company

10th Mechanized Infantry Brigade – Brig. Gen. Joffre
3rd Mechanized Infantry Regiment
6th Mechanized Infantry Regiment
7th Mechanized Infantry Regiment
A Company, 1st Infantry Regiment
Airlifted Artillery Group 4
10th Mechanized Logistics Battalion
10th Armoured Cavalry Reconnaissance Squadron
10th Mechanized Sapper (Engineer) Company
10th Mechanized Communications Company
10th Mechanized Company of Electronic Operations
　　(Signals)
10th Mechanized Medical Company

Argentine Naval and Marines units
Detachment of Buzos Tácticos (Naval Special Forces, akin to US Navy SEALS or UK Special Boat Service)
1 x Platoon, 1st Marine Infantry Battalion
2nd Marine Infantry Battalion
H Company, 3rd Marine Infantry Battalion
5th Marine Infantry Battalion
Battery A, Field Artillery Battalion of Marine Infantry
Battery B, Field Artillery Battalion of Marine Infantry
Company of Amphibious Commandos
Marine Infantry Anti-Aircraft Battalion
Company of Amphibious Sappers/Marine Infantry
Heavy Machine-Gun Company 12.7/Marine Infantry

Argentine Air Force units

Squadrons 1 and 2, Anti-aircraft Artillery

Special Operations Group

School of Military Aviation

Principal Argentine deployments in the Falklands:

Stanley (approx. 8,400 personnel)

Goose Green (approx. 1,200 personnel)

Port Howard, West Falkland (approx. 800 personnel)

Fox Bay, West Falkland (approx. 900 personnel)

Pebble Island, off West Falkland (approx. 120 personnel)

BRITISH GROUND FORCES IN THE FALKLANDS, SOUTH GEORGIA AND ON ASCENSION (c.7,000 PERSONNEL)

3 Commando Brigade Royal Marines – Brigadier Julian Thompson, RM

    40 Commando RM

    42 Commando RM

    45 Commando RM

    29 (Commando) Regiment, RA

    148 Commando FO Battery, RA

    59 Independent Commando Squadron, RM

    Commando Logistic Regiment, RM

    3 Commando Brigade HQ & Signals Squadron, RM

    3 Commando Brigade Air Squadron, RM

    1 Raiding Squadron, RM

    2, 4 and 6 Sections, Special Boat Squadron, RM

    Mountain and Arctic Warfare Cadre, RM

    Nos. 845 and 846 Naval Air Squadrons

    Landing Ships Logistic and Mexefloat Detachments

    Y Troop, RM Signals

    49 Explosive Ordnance Device Squadron, RE

    Surgical Support Team, RN

    Commando Forces Band, RM (tasked with medical duties)

Army units attached to 3 Commando Bde

    3rd Battalion The Parachute Regiment

    Medium Recce Troop, B Squadron, The Blues and Royals

    T Battery, 12 Air Defence Regiment, RA

    FOO Parties, 4 Field Regiment, RA

    RLD, 30 Signals Regiment, Royal Signals

    Section, 19 Field Ambulance, RAMC/RADC

5 Infantry Brigade – Brig. M. J. A. Wilson

    2nd Battalion The Scots Guards

    1st Battalion The Welsh Guards

    2nd Battalion The Parachute Regiment

    1st Battalion 7th Gurkha Rifles

    4 Field Regiment, RA

    2 Troops, 32 Guided Weapons Regiment, RA

FOO Parties, 49 Field Regiment, Royal School of Artillery

Support Regiment, RA

36 Engineer Regiment, RE

9 Para Squadron, RE

Detachment, 2 Port Control Regiment, RE

No. 656 Squadron, Army Air Corp

407 Transport Troop, Royal Corps of Transport

Elements, 17 Port Regiment, RCT

16 Field Ambulance, RAMC

81 Ordnance Company, RAOC

Laundry/Bakery Detachment, 9 Ordnance Battalion, RAOC

Elms, 421 EOD Company, RAOC/RE

10 Forward Workshop, REME

160 Provo Company, Royal Military Police

6 Field Cash Office, Royal Army Pay Corps

Force Troops

Army Elms., HQ LFFI

12 Air Defence Regiment, RA

21 Air Defence Battery, 27 Field Regiment, RA

11 Squadron, 38 Engineer Regiment, RE

Detachment, 38 Engineer Regiment, RE

Detachment, 2 PC Regiment, RE

Elements, Military Works Force, RPC

Detachment, 11 Ordnance Battalion, RAOC

Detachment, 14 Signals Regiment, Royal Signals

Detachments., 30 Signals Regiment, Royal Signals

D and G Squadrons, 22 SAS Regiment.

Elements, No. 657 Squadron, AAC

172 Intelligence and Security Section, Intelligence Corps

Elements, 17 Port Regiment, RCT

Elements, Joint Helicopter Service Unit, RAF

Elements, 29 Moving Regiment, Royal Corps of Transport/REME

Ascension Island

Elements, 22 Engineer Regiment, RE

Elements, 38 Engineer Regiment, RE

Elements, Mil. Works Force, RPC

Detachment, 2 PC Regiment, RE

Detachment, 30 Signals Regiment, Royal Signals

47 Air Despatch Squadron, RCT

Laundry Detachment, 9 Ordnance Battalion, RAOC

Detachment, 4 Petrol Depot, RAOC

Detachment, 49 Rp Company

Misc. RAOC, ACC

Note: A study devoted exclusively to land operations cannot ignore the role played by warships and aircraft, particularly in an expeditionary operation of this kind which decisively depended upon support by air and sea. While the nature and scope of this work must by necessity exclude exhaustive coverage of air and naval assets, the role they played in numerous tasks in the South Atlantic cannot go unmentioned, such as excluding the Argentine Navy from the theatre of operations, providing air cover, landing special forces, conducting shore bombardment during the landings at San Carlos and support to ground operations thereafter; escorting troop and supply ships, offering them protection from Argentine aircraft, surface vessel and submarine attack, and serving as command, control and communications platforms. Helicopter squadrons, consisting of Sea Kings, Wessex Lynx and Wasps served aboard warships, and RAF Chinooks transported troops and stores. Sea Harriers and Hercules transports, Nimrod reconnaissance aircraft, Vulcan bombers, Victor tankers, Phantom fighters and units of the RAF Regiment also took part. A range of vessels, including aircraft carriers, submarines, Royal Fleet Auxiliary vessels, destroyers, frigates, tankers, minesweepers, hospital ships, merchantmen naturally played an indispensable part in the operations.

OPPOSING PLANS

ARGENTINE PLANS

The Argentine plan calculated – wrongly in the event – on Britain declining to oppose the armed occupation of the Falklands, with President Galtieri gambling on the United Nations demanding a negotiated settlement of the dispute and Britain accepting the occupation as a fait accompli. The islands' isolation, modest financial value based principally on fisheries and sheep farming, poor strategic situation and tiny population of 1,800 inhabitants all appeared to militate against an armed response to Argentine occupation. In any event strategists in Buenos Aires reckoned the distance to be too great for Britain to be able to mount an expeditionary operation when her NATO commitments required the bulk of her land forces and air assets in Germany, and her fleet in the North Atlantic.

Argentina's historical claim to the islands dated back to the early 19th century and enjoyed the support of some of her South American neighbours, though not, significantly, Chile, with whom Galtieri's government maintained a frosty relationship on the basis of several contentious issues, including a long-standing territorial dispute over Tierra del Fuego. Significantly, this obliged Argentina to withhold some of its best troops to observe the Chileans along an extremely lengthy frontier. Barring an unexpected armed response by Britain, this posed no serious disruption to Argentine plans to occupy the Falklands. The invasion proper was be preceded by a token force exercising a claim on the bleak, uninhabited dependency of South Georgia by subterfuge. An Argentine businessman, Constantino Davidoff, contracted through the Scottish company of Christian Salvesen, acquired permission to remove scrap metal left behind by the defunct whaling industry. By dispatching Davidoff and a party of workers with the intention of raising the Argentine flag and laying claim to a territory with no permanent residents, Argentina intended to set a precedent for occupation of the larger prize: the Falklands themselves.

Having secured South Georgia, the Argentines planned to launch Operation *Rosario*, involving multiple landings on West and East Falkland, with the Buzos Tácticos to attack both the Royal Marines barracks at Moody Brook and Government House, overwhelm the small garrison and oblige it rapidly to surrender. The 2nd Marine Battalion, landed by the ships of Task Group 40.1, would support this operation if called upon. With the airfield secured by the marines forming the initial invasion force, a small garrison of army personnel would be airlifted into Stanley at a later stage. The Argentines planned to occupy the islands with no more than a brigade, but once the Task Force left Britain the garrison would eventually grow to over 11,000 strong – a force difficult to supply at a distance of 400 miles (650km) if Britain were to succeed in establishing an effective naval blockade and dominance in the air. The majority of these troops, some 8,000, remained in and around Stanley where they constituted a reinforced brigade drawn from five regiments, along with artillery anti-aircraft batteries, armoured car and engineer units. Over 1,000 infantry with anti-aircraft capability and some artillery were deployed to Goose Green, while on West Falkland, two garrisons, each of approximately 800 men, occupied Port Howard and Fox Bay, together with engineer support.

Once her initial plan of establishing a small military presence in the Falklands became unsustainable, Argentina adopted long-term plans involving troops of sufficient number to withstand efforts by Britain to repossess the islands. Within a month of the initial landings on 2 April, the Argentines had established a massive military presence, with infantry backed by associated supporting arms, helicopters, field guns, anti-aircraft batteries and logistic support. Within the first week of April the Argentines had established Pucará and Mentor fighter aircraft and Tracker anti-submarine aircraft in the Stanley area and by the end of the month had rendered operational the grass airstrip on Pebble Island, off West Falkland, together with that at Goose Green on East Falkland.

BRITISH PLANS

In military terms, restoring the Falklands to British rule represented an exceedingly daunting task. The islands lie approximately 8,000 miles (7,000 nautical miles, 13,000km) from the United Kingdom and consist of the two main islands of West and East Falkland, with another 100 smaller islands – covering between them over 4,700 square miles, or two-thirds the area of Wales. Their landscape and climate resemble that of the western isles of

British Chiefs of Staff grouped around the conference table at the Ministry of Defence in London during the Falklands War. Left to right: Admiral Sir Henry Leach (First Sea Lord and Chief of the Naval Staff); Admiral Sir Terence Lewin (Chief of the Defence Staff); General Sir Edwin Bramall (Chief of the General Staff); Sir Frank Cooper (Permanent Under Secretary of State, Ministry of Defence); and Professor Sir Ronald Mason (Chief Scientific Adviser to the Ministry of Defence). (Imperial War Museum, FKD 2601)

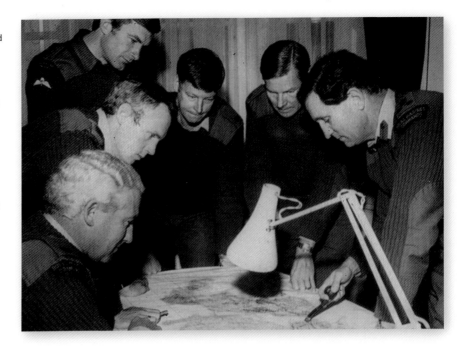

Part of the planning team whose responsibilities included choosing the most suitable landing site for 3 Commando Brigade. Chief amongst their considerations were undefended beaches with firm sand, a protected anchorage and sufficient space for the landing force to expand the beachhead. Major Southby-Tailyour, who possessed an intimate knowledge of the coastline, stands at left while Brig. Thompson stands at right identifying a position with a pipe. (Royal Marines Museum)

Scotland and consist largely of boggy, undulating moorland and windswept rocky outcrops, almost bereft of trees. Extremely isolated, the Falklands form the only major island group in the South Atlantic and lie 300 miles (500km) east of the Strait of Magellan, with a climate suitably inclement. The temperature varies between 49 degrees Fahrenheit (9 degrees Celsius) in January – which of course represents the height of summer in the southern hemisphere – and 36 degrees Fahrenheit (2 degrees Celsius) in July, which conversely marks the depth of winter. From a military perspective such a distinctive, changeable and, depending on the season, harsh climate requires troops to be well protected. Troops improperly equipped, clothed, fed or unaccustomed to operating in these unforgiving conditions could not be expected to function in an effective manner – a point which bitter experience was soon to confirm.

Stanley, the capital and only town in this overseas territory, sits on the east coast of East Falkland and represented the ultimate objective of British forces. Its 1,000 residents accounted for more than half the entire population of the islands, with the other 800 living in widely scattered settlements in the 'camp' unconnected by road, though in some cases airstrips offered limited access. Retaking the Falklands appeared to planners in London to depend partly on early success against the small Argentine garrison on South Georgia, a 100-mile-long (160km) island lying 900 miles (1,500km) east-south-east of the Falklands. Retaking the island would not only boost morale even before the main landings took place in the Falklands themselves, but provide a safe haven for troopships – particularly those rapidly acquired from civilian use, like the luxury liner *QE2*. Once safely ensconced in the waters around Grytviken men and supplies could be transferred by 'cross-decking' to military vessels with at least limited air cover provided by the carriers and escort by warship.

The British had by necessity to operate along a lengthy chain of command, with the Secretary of State for Defence, John Nott, reporting to his staff in London, led by the Chief of the Defence Staff (CDS), Admiral of the Fleet Sir

Terence Lewin and other service heads. The Task Force Commanders, under the Commander-in-Chief Fleet, Admiral Sir John Fieldhouse, worked at Northwood, Middlesex, near London. Fieldhouse would control military and naval affairs in the South Atlantic via the various commanders *in situ*: Rear Admiral J. F. 'Sandy' Woodward, commander of the Carrier Battle Group, Commander Michael Clapp, commander of the Amphibious Task Group, and Brigadier Julian Thompson RM, commander of the Landing Force Task Group and 3 Commando Brigade.

Recapturing the islands would require a strategy based on stages. The principal military objectives involved imposing a sea blockade around the Falklands; retaking South Georgia to make use of it as a secure base and transit area; establishing air and naval supremacy around the Falklands; and, lastly, defeating the Argentine garrison on the Falklands and reoccupying the islands. All this required use of Ascension Island, which stood approximately halfway between Britain and the Falklands – about 4,000 miles (6,500km). With its American-built runway at Wideawake Airfield, Ascension could accommodate all aircraft, especially those carrying vital supplies for the Task Force; serve as an intermediary base for stores and fuel; and permit cross-decking and the reloading of supplies already embarked on the island.

Whatever plan the British devised, time was of the essence. The UN could call a ceasefire and place Britain in an awkward diplomatic position if she refused to comply. Even if diplomatic obstacles and all the logistical problems associated with the prosecution of a campaign 8,000 miles (13,000km) away could be overcome, autumnal conditions in the South Atlantic would imminently take a turn for the worse. With the approach of winter, and with well over a month before a task force could reach the islands and carry out a successful landing, the temperature would have dropped and precipitation increased. Even if ground forces could operate, their progress would be hindered by heavy seas, conditions rendering all but impossible the launching of sorties from the swaying decks of aircraft carriers, the cross-decking of troops and supplies between vessels pitching amidst the swells, and would eventually disrupt or sever general resupply – not to mention cause serious problems for airborne anti-submarine surveillance and the ability to launch defensive air sorties to protect vital maritime assets.

To compound these already formidable problems, given the Argentines' superior numbers, firepower and defensive posture, executing an amphibious landing depended heavily on the ability of the task force to come ashore unopposed while its supporting craft established a secure and sheltered anchorage. The size of the expeditionary force would also require an area large enough to enable an oversized brigade to establish a strong bridgehead. Heavy casualties – at least at such an early stage in the campaign – could not be tolerated given the uncertain nature of the British public's appetite for a costly war conducted for a distant and remote territory whose occupation by Argentina, however unpalatable, constituted no threat to British security at home. In any event, a contested landing would without doubt slow the breakout and subsequent advance on Stanley, while the troops (hardened though they were) would be condemned to operate in the extremely inhospitable conditions of a rapidly approaching Antarctic winter. In short, the campaign had by necessity to be short, sharp and decisive, with a high tempo maintained throughout and success achieved with minimum casualties – daunting requirements for a nation which had not conducted a large-scale amphibious operation since the landings at Suez in 1956.

THE CAMPAIGN

ARGENTINE OPERATIONS AGAINST SOUTH GEORGIA AND THE FALKLANDS, 19 MARCH TO 3 APRIL

South Georgia, a dependency of the Falklands covering 1,450 square miles, is dominated by mountain ranges and glaciers, with conditions similar to the Antarctic. It had no permanent residents – only the approximately two-dozen staff of the British Antarctic Survey (BAS) who worked at King Edward Point near the abandoned whaling station at Grytviken. As a dependency of the Falklands, South Georgia comprised part of Argentina's general claim to British possessions which included the extremely remote, uninhabited South Sandwich Islands. The Argentines organized the occupation of South Georgia by stealth, arriving under the pretext of conducting a commercial operation authorized by the British government via its embassy in Buenos Aires. This arrangement permitted workmen to salvage scrap metal from the former whaling enterprise across several sites on the island, particularly at Leith and the main settlement, Grytviken.

A small group of workmen duly arrived aboard the fleet transport *Bahiá Buen Suceso* on 19 March, but they commenced work without conforming to the requirement of reporting first to the island's magistrate, the Base Commander of the British Antarctic Survey (BAS) based at King Edward Point near Grytviken. The workmen raised the Argentine flag and, despite being called upon, refused to obtain proper authorization for their presence. At the same time, the ice patrol ship HMS *Endurance* – the only Royal Navy vessel present in South Atlantic waters, entered Stanley Harbour en route to Britain, her tour of duty in the South Atlantic having reached its end. On word of events on South Georgia, however, Fleet HQ in Northwood, near London, ordered *Endurance* to reverse course and make for South Georgia with her complement of 13 Royal Marines, plus nine more from the Falklands garrison of Navy Party 8901 which, by annual rotation of personnel, had furnished a protection force to the Falklands for the past 30 years. While diplomatic efforts got under way between Britain and Argentina to settle the dispute, the Argentine transport departed, leaving a complement of the civilian workers. *Endurance* reached Grytviken on 23 March, evacuated the BAS team from Leith and inserted Royal Marines by Wasp helicopter.

No attempt was made to remove the scrap metal workers during the continuing phase of negotiations between Britain and Argentina, but the latter dispatched the icebreaker *Bahía Paraíso* to protect them, and on 25 March she arrived at Leith, disembarking about a hundred marines under Lt. Cdr. Alfredo Astiz. The situation escalated when, on 31 March, with negotiations deadlocked, *Endurance* landed a detachment of Royal Marines at King Edward Point to establish a defensive position. She then left Cumberland Bay, unobserved by *Bahía Paraíso*, and made for Stanley. When, two days later, the Argentines occupied that town as part of the descent on the Falklands themselves, *Endurance* altered course and headed back towards South Georgia. In the meantime, the Argentine frigate *Guerrico* had left the mainland to rendezvous with *Bahía Paraíso* as Task Force 60.

On 3 April, both Argentine vessels, with many of the marines re-embarked from Leith, anchored off Grytviken and radioed the magistrate with a call to surrender. He, in turn, devolved authority upon Lt. Mills of the Royal Marines, who prepared to resist. Fighting began around noon, when an Argentine Puma from *Bahía Paraíso* landed about 20 men near King Edward Point. A second journey by the Puma, laden with marines, came under fire from the Royal Marines, who, though equipped with only small arms, badly damaged the helicopter just off the Point, killing two Argentines and forcing the stricken helicopter to lift off. The Puma only reached the other side of King Edward Cove before crashing, although the Argentines continued to make use of an Alouette to ferry in more marines. But the defenders faced poor odds, for *Guerrico* approached the shore in support of the landings and commenced firing on Mills's positions, prompting his men to direct their fire – small arms plus 66mm Light Anti-tank Weapons (LAWs) and 84s (Carl Gustav medium anti-tank weapon) – causing *Guerrico* to reverse course away from shore.

From her new position, she directed the fire of her 100mm gun against the garrison while Argentine marines began to encircle Mills's position by moving around the cover provided by the whaling station at Grytviken. Finding himself surrounded, with one man wounded and the satisfaction that he had at least offered sufficient resistance to justify the decision, Mills surrendered his force of 22 marines and the 13 British civilians at Grytviken. *Endurance* arrived later the same day, but obviously too late to take part in the engagement. She remained in South Georgia waters for two more days before sailing north on 5 April with orders to link up with the vanguard of the British task force then assembling at Portsmouth and Southampton.

The Argentines organized the build-up for their invasion of their principal objective, the Falklands, during the period of Anglo-Argentine negotiations which followed the landing on South Georgia that began on 19 March. With talks failing to make headway, Argentina initiated Operation *Rosario*, dispatching ships south, their destination unknown to British intelligence, but by the 31st observers in London assumed that in light of events on South Georgia an invasion was imminent and warned the islands' governor, Rex Hunt. On the evening of 1 April he therefore announced by radio the likelihood of invasion occurring the following day, while in the meantime the garrison of the islands, a mere 70 Royal Marines of Naval Party 8901 under Maj. Mike Norman, who, anticipating that the main landing would take place near Stanley airfield with a subsequent advance on the town, deployed his men into four delaying sections along the Stanley road, with his main force concentrated at Government House.

The Argentines landed at several sites in the early hours of 2 April, with a party of Buzos Tácticos landed by the destroyer *Santísima Trinidad* and

Argentine landings, 1–2 April

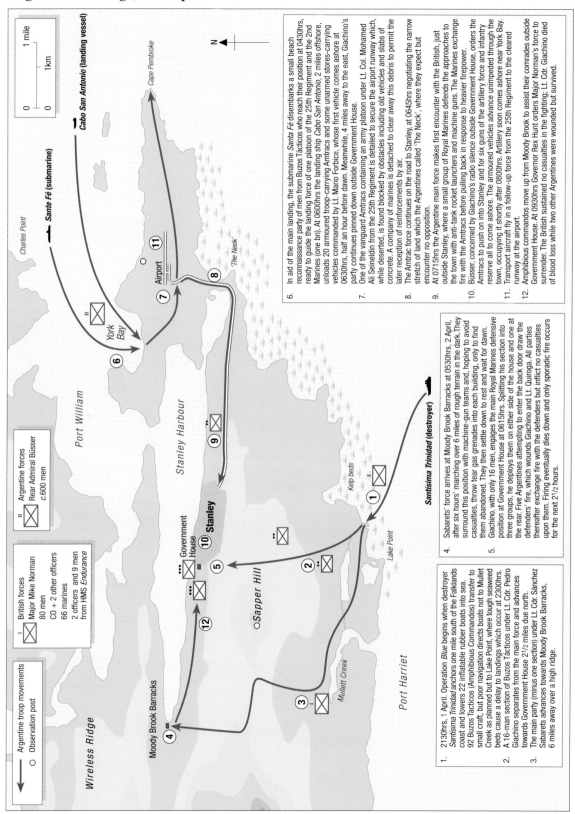

Key / Legend boxes:

Argentine troop movements

○ Observation post

British forces
Major Mike Norman
80 men
CO + 2 other officers
66 marines
2 officers and 9 men
from HMS *Endurance*

Argentine forces
Rear Admiral Büsser
c.600 men

Scale: 0 – 1 mile / 0 – 1km

N

Map labels:

Cape Pembroke

Cabo San Antonio (landing vessel)

Sante Fé (submarine)

Charles Point

York Bay

Airport

'The Neck'

Port William

Stanley Harbour

Kelp beds

Government House

Stanley

Sapper Hill

Lake Point

Wireless Ridge

Moody Brook Barracks

Mullett Creek

Santisima Trinidad (destroyer)

Port Harriet

Numbered notes:

1. 2130hrs, 1 April. Operation *Blue* begins when destroyer *Santísima Trinidad* anchors one mile south of the Falklands coast and lowers 22 inflatable rubber boats into sea. 92 Buzos Tácticos (Amphibious Commandos) transfer to small craft, but poor navigation directs boats not to Mullet Creek as planned but to Lake Point, where tough seaweed beds cause a delay to landings which occur at 2300hrs. A 16-man section of Buzos Tácticos under Lt. Cdr. Pedro Giachino separates from the main force and advances towards Government House 2½ miles due north.

2. The main party (minus one section) under Lt. Cdr. Sánchez Sabarets advances towards Moody Brook Barracks, 6 miles away over a high ridge.

3. [blank]

4. Sabarets' force arrives at Moody Brook Barracks at 0530hrs, 2 April, after six hours' marching over 6 miles of rough terrain in the dark. They surround this position with machine-gun teams and, hoping to avoid casualties, throw tear gas grenades into each building, only to find them abandoned. They then settle down to rest and wait for dawn.

5. Giachino, with only 16 men, engages the main Royal Marines defensive position at Government House at 0615hrs. Splitting his section into three groups, he deploys them on either side of the house and one at the rear. Five Argentines attempting to enter the back door draw the defenders' fire, which wounds Giachino and Lt. Quiroga. All parties thereafter exchange fire with the defenders but inflict no casualties upon them. Firing eventually dies down and only sporadic fire occurs for the next 2½ hours.

6. In aid of the main landing, the submarine *Santa Fé* disembarks a small beach reconnaissance party of men from Buzos Tácticos who reach their position at 0430hrs, ready to guide the landing force of one platoon of the 25th Regiment and the 2nd Marines (one bn). At 0600hrs the landing ship *Cabo San Antonio*, 2 miles offshore, unloads 20 armoured troop-carrying Amtracs and some unarmed stores-carrying vehicles commanded by Lt. Mario Forbice, whose first vehicle comes ashore at 0630hrs, half an hour before dawn. Meanwhile, 4 miles away to the east, Giachino's party continues pinned down outside Government House.

7. One of the vanguard Amtracs containing an army platoon under Lt. Col. Mohamed Alí Seinaldín from the 25th Regiment is detailed to secure the airport runway which, while deserted, is found blocked by obstacles including old vehicles and slabs of concrete. A company of marines is detached to clear away this debris to permit the later reception of reinforcements by air.

8. The Amtrac force continues on the road to Stanley, at 0645hrs negotiating the narrow stretch of land which the Argentines called 'The Neck', where they expect but encounter no opposition.

9. At 0715hrs the Argentine main force makes first encounter with the British, just outside Stanley, where a small group of Royal Marines defends the approaches to the town with anti-tank rocket launchers and machine guns. The Marines exchange fire with the Amtracs before pulling back in response to heavier firepower.

10. Busser, concerned by Giachino's radio silence outside Government House, orders the Amtracs to push on into Stanley and for six guns of the artillery force and infantry reserve all to come ashore. The armoured vehicles advance unimpeded through the town, occupying it shortly after 0800hrs. Artillery soon comes ashore near York Bay.

11. Transport aircraft fly in a follow-up force from the 25th Regiment to the cleared runway at the airport.

12. Amphibious commandos move up from Moody Brook to assist their comrades outside Government House. At 0930hrs Governor Rex Hunt orders Major Norman's force to surrender. The British sustained no casualties in the fighting; Lt. Cdr. Giachino died of blood loss while two other Argentines were wounded but survived.

occupying Mullet Creek while another group went ashore from the submarine *Santa Fé* to inspect the main landing beach north of Stanley. At 0430hrs more commandos landed at Mullet Creek by helicopter, probably from the icebreaker *Almirante Irizar*, with the majority of these forces en route for the barracks at Moody Brook, which the Royal Marines had wisely abandoned. Other Argentine units proceeded north of Sapper Hill with Stanley as their objective. Meanwhile, destroyers and frigates of Task Force 40, lying off Stanley, assumed support positions and a landing craft (LST) approached the undefended beach at York Bay. At 0600hrs the main assault and supporting landings began, with the principal force of Buzos Tácticos reaching Moody Brook before proceeding east towards Government House on the western fringe of the town. There, the defenders were already under attack from the small force but holding firm. At approximately 0630hrs, the Argentines began to land their first armoured vehicles from the *Cabo San Antonio*, including about 20 LVTP-7 Amtracs carrying 20 marines each,

TOP LEFT
Argentine marine of the 601st Marine Commando Company wearing camouflage face paint and carrying grenades and a mortar. His unit spearheaded the attack after landing from the destroyer *Santísima Trinidad* at 2130hrs on 1 April. (Imperial War Museum, FKD 2177)

TOP RIGHT
Royal Marines of Naval Party (NP) 8901 detained as prisoners outside Government House, where a marine of the 601st Marine Commando Company, the unit which captured them, stands guard. (Imperial War Museum, FKD 2193)

LEFT
Argentine marines. Parts of four battalions served in the Falklands: a platoon-sized group from the 1st Marines seized South Georgia; 390 men from 2nd Marines landed on 2 April at York Bay and occupied Stanley; 3rd Marines divided its companies between Stanley, Pebble Island and Goose Green; and 5th Marines arrived in late April and occupied Mt Tumbledown, Mt William and Sapper Hill. (Imperial War Museum, FKD 2192)

followed 15 minutes later by more troops arriving at the airfield by helicopter. Those Royal Marine detachments outside Government House, finding themselves unable to resist the assault, fell back to the main position, with one section managing to disable an Amtrac with its anti-armour weapons. Meanwhile, the main body of the Argentine garrison, principally from 25th Infantry Regiment, arrived at Stanley airfield totally unopposed.

By dawn Argentine forces had surrounded Government House and kept it under constant small-arms fire, with the Amtracs approaching in support. Unable to resist such overwhelming numbers and firepower, Governor Hunt ordered the marines to surrender, which duly took place at 0915hrs, by which time they had inflicted several casualties on their attackers whilst suffering none themselves. Command of the garrison fell initially on Lt. Gen. Osvaldo Garcia, but on 7 April, Brig. Gen. Mario Menéndez assumed that responsibility as both Commander-in-Chief of the 'Malvinas' and Military Governor. On the same day, Britain declared a 200-nautical mile (370km) maritime exclusion zone (MEZ) around the Falklands, with effect from the 12th. By the 5th, most of the warships had in fact returned to ports in Argentina, although the build-up of troops and stores continued via the fleet transport vessel *Bahía Buen Suceso* and the merchantmen *Formosa* and *Rio Carcarana*, together with transport aircraft. On the very day of the invasion, the United Nations adopted Resolution 502, ordering the withdrawal of all Argentine forces; two days later, on 4 April, it condemned the occupation as an act of aggression.

INITIAL BRITISH RESPONSE: SOUTH GEORGIA AND PEBBLE ISLAND, 21–28 APRIL AND 14 MAY

The Task Force engaged in the effort to restore control over South Georgia, known as Operation *Paraquet*, included HM submarine *Conqueror*, the destroyer HMS *Antrim* and the Royal Fleet Auxiliary vessel *Tidespring*, and arrived off South Georgia on the morning of 21 April, with no Argentine ships spotted by air or naval reconnaissance over the previous two days. Operations commenced with the establishment of observation posts by the Special Air Service (SAS) near Leith and by the Special Boat Squadron (SBS) south of Grytviken. Mountain Troop, SAS, arrived by three Wessex helicopters on Fortuna Glacier around noon, but the troop encountered high winds and freezing conditions overnight and when helicopters returned the following morning to evacuate them amidst dreadful flying conditions, difficulties in negotiating the glacier so extended their time in the air and taxed their engines as to oblige them to return for refuelling. In the second attempt the men came away successfully, but extremely poor visibility led two Wessex to crash, with a third managing first to offload its contingent before eventually reaching the remaining men and carrying them away that afternoon in an extremely crowded and overloaded manner. Two Lynx helicopters from the frigate HMS *Brilliant* were then drafted in to compensate for the downed Wessex from *Antrim*.

Late on the following evening, the 22nd, SAS Boat Troop, dispatched from *Antrim* in Stromness Bay, proceeded to Grass Island, but as before with disastrous consequences; two of the five Gemini assault craft which proceeded in the darkness broke down and required rescue the following morning by *Antrim*'s Wessex, which located one crew but failed to locate the second, whose rescue beacon was not switched on until after the island was retaken. Still, on the 23rd the SAS team reached its objectives. At the same time the SBS

landed at Hound Bay from HMS *Endurance* early on the morning of the 22nd, struggled in their approach to Grytviken and proceeded across Sorling Valley before unsuccessfully attempting to cross Cumberland Bay East in Gemini boats. Glacier ice prevented them from making the crossing, forcing them to remain *in situ* until collected later by Wasp on the 24th.

When the task group, including *Tidespring* and *Antrim*, learned of the approach of the submarine *Santa Fé* into Grytviken with troops and stores the threat obliged the vessels to leave South Georgia's waters, apart from *Endurance* which remained behind hugging the coast amidst the ice fields. With the task group went the main landing force of M Coy, 42 Commando, aboard *Tidespring* which, once safely distant from submarine menace, enabled HMS *Antrim*, *Plymouth* and *Brilliant* to engage the Argentine submarine. The *Santa Fé* was observed on the morning of 25 April off Cumberland Bay and damaged by a combination of fire from helicopters, *Endurance* and *Plymouth*, forcing the stricken vessel to struggle into Grytviken harbour.

With the growing threat posed by the return of the *Santa Fé* and the desire to engage the garrison as quickly as possible, the British placed a high priority on the recovery of South Georgia and duly dispatched a landing force under the cover of naval gunfire, without the reinforcements still available on *Tidespring* in the form of most of M Coy. A composite company of 75 men gathered from the SAS, SBS and Royal Marines was assembled to confront the approximately 140-man garrison. In the afternoon, *Antrim* and *Plymouth* directed naval support fire from their 4.5in. guns against the Argentine positions at King Edward Point. The first contingent of the makeshift British force arrived by *Antrim*'s Wessex and *Brilliant*'s two Lynx at Hestesletten on the 27th, from where they advanced through the whaling station at Grytviken before – unbeknownst to them – entering a minefield in the direction of the BAS base. Observing their approach, the Argentines produced white flags and surrendered, without any exchange of fire, around 1700hrs. When called upon by radio to surrender his small detachment of marines at Leith, Astiz refused to do so, whereupon the next morning, the 28th, *Endurance* and *Plymouth* sailed to Leith, where their unexpected presence convinced the

REAR ADMIRAL BÜSSER PREPARING TO OPEN NEGOTIATIONS, GOVERNMENT HOUSE, 2 APRIL (pp. 32–33)

Rear Admiral Carlos Büsser (1), Landing Force Commander, accompanied by a subordinate officer (2) and a commando (3) confer with a Royal Marine (4) before meeting Major Mike Norman, RM, and Governor Rex Hunt. Despite several hours' resistance during which time, totally surrounded, his tiny force wounded three commandos and killed the crew of an Amtrac, Norman understood that it was only a matter of time before the Argentines brought up massive reinforcements. In due course these arrived on East Falkland in the form of helicopters, support weapons and mortars, more armoured vehicles and several hundred infantry. By 0900hrs, with surrender still out of the question, three options remained: break out, with the governor, in the process incurring some casualties; remain *in situ* and continue resistance, recognizing nevertheless that mounting enemy numbers and firepower spelt inevitable defeat; or, finally, attempt to negotiate a truce. Contact was made with Argentine HQ via Hector Gilobert, an ex-Argentine Air Force officer who ran civilian flights between the mainland and the Falklands.

Hoping to negotiate a ceasefire rather than to surrender, and fearing that his departure from the building would signify the latter, Hunt dispatched Dick Baker, the Chief Secretary, together with the summoned Gilobert, to make contact with Büsser via a radio broadcast relayed from the nearby police station. Büsser and two others duly appeared at the Town Hall and proceeded to Government House, where on the lawn, shown here, he requested permission to enter the building. On doing so he shook hands with a number of soldiers, though Hunt refused on the grounds that Büsser constituted an intruder. The governor offered a truce only in order for the three Argentine wounded, still lying unattended outside, to be collected, and insisted that Büsser withdraw his forces from the islands. Büsser, of course, held all the cards, and informed the defiant governor that in light of the fall of Moody Brook Barracks, the airport, the whole of Stanley apart from Government House and, above all, the attackers' overwhelming numerical superiority, the only sensible option for Hunt was to surrender, his men having acquitted themselves honourably against hopeless odds. Further resistance, the admiral continued, would leave him no option but to continue fighting, with dire consequences to life and property, upon which Hunt ordered the Marines to lay down their arms. The Falklands were now in Argentine hands.

Soldiers of 2 Para aboard the ferry *Norland* stand by for transfer to landing craft which will take them ashore at San Carlos. (Imperial War Museum, FKD 851)

defenders that they had no option but to lay down their arms. M Coy, 42 Commando, remained behind – much to their disappointment – to garrison South Georgia, with *Endurance* stationed as guard ship.

BRITISH LANDINGS AT SAN CARLOS, 21 MAY

Admiral Woodward and his subordinates well appreciated that every effort was to be made to ensure the protection of the landing force and its supporting vessels from air attack. While air and naval operations fall outside the confines of this work, ground forces played their part in this effort to bring Thompson's force safely to shore; specifically, a dramatic raid conducted by D Squadron, 22 SAS, on the small grass airstrip on Pebble Island, just north of West Falkland, from which the Argentines could potentially harass the landings using ground-attack Pucarás and other aircraft based there. On the night of 11 May men from Boat Troop went ashore undetected to reconnoitre the area and determine the strength of the garrison, and the best method of approach. Three days later, the aircraft carrier HMS *Hermes* and her escort the frigate HMS *Broadsword*, with *Glamorgan* in fire support, approached Pebble Island at night, putting *Glamorgan*'s guns within range of the airstrip. Meanwhile, from aboard *Hermes*, 48 SAS troopers and a naval gunfire support team flew off in Sea King helicopters, guided into position by the patrol already in place on the ground.

After a rapid march to the airstrip, D Squadron launched its attack, supported by fire from *Glamorgan*, as described by Sergeant Peter Ratcliffe:

> On the airstrip... it rapidly became apparent that the Argentinians had effectively abandoned any attempt to save the aircraft and were lying low, looking out for their own safety and hardly firing back at all. A single brave enemy officer and one of his soldiers did try to stop the raiding teams, opening fire on them, but they were quickly shot down. It was then that Mountain Troop began using the few explosive charges they had to wreck the rest of the aircraft.

To reach the wings of some of the machines they had to stand on each other's shoulders; once the first man had scrambled up he would reach down and pull the other guy up after him. The Pucarás – twin-turboprop ground-attack aircraft – were the tallest planes and caused the demolition teams the most trouble.

By this time the pre-dawn sky was glowing orange from fires raging in the Argentinians' fuel store, which had been hit by *Glamorgan*'s guns. Then the destroyer's gunners found the range for the enemy's ammunition dump and blew it to smithereens. As the final charges shattered the last of the aircraft, the squadron began to withdraw.

The raid – very much conducted in the tradition of those conducted by the SAS in North Africa during World War II – proved an overwhelming success; in all, the Argentines lost six Pucarás, four Mentors and one Skyvan, as well as the use of the airstrip just a week before the task force intended to put ashore 3 Commando Brigade, supporting elements and a vast array of supplies.

The vessels involved in the landings in San Carlos Water represented the largest contingent of amphibious shipping since the Suez operation of 1956. In all, it comprised the Amphibious Assault Ships *Fearless* and *Intrepid*, five LSLs, the liner *Canberra* and two ferries, *Norland* and *Europic Ferry*, which would convey the landing force, with support provided by the destroyer *Antrim* and the frigates *Broadsword*, *Ardent*, *Brilliant*, *Antelope*, *Argonaut*, *Plymouth* and *Yarmouth*, all present in Falkland Sound. Troop-carrying Sea King helicopters operated out of the RFAs *Stromness* and *Fort Austin* nearby. The aircraft carriers *Hermes* and *Invincible* and their escorts further out to sea would provide air cover, though Admiral Woodward explicitly warned Thompson and Clapp that not only could he provide no guarantee of air superiority over the landing area – he could not bring his carriers close inshore since the Harriers would be needed to defend his ships from Argentine aircraft.

Brigadier Thompson issued orders for the landings, codenamed Operation *Sutton*, on 13 May aboard *Fearless* while still 1,000 miles (1,600km) from the Falklands. These encapsulated Moore's directive of the previous day calling for the establishment of a secure bridgehead which allowed reinforcements to land, to move forward as far as security could be maintained and to 'establish moral and physical domination over the enemy'. The precise date and time of the landings had yet to be decided. As discussed, the following day the SAS carried out its highly successful raid against Pebble Island. Special Forces again showed their value just prior to the landings when, in response to reports of a small number of Argentines operating on Fanning Head overlooking San Carlos Water to the north, a heavily armed team of 25 men from the SBS was landed on the night of the 20th – the day before D-Day – to neutralize the potential threat which defenders armed with anti-tank or similar weapons would pose to the lightly armoured landing craft.

H-Hour was established for 0230hrs local time on 21 May. The transport vessels anchored off San Carlos Water around 2300hrs on the 20th, supported by the warships, and began embarking troops into their landing craft shortly after midnight, with 40 Commando and 2 Para forming the first wave. H-Hour was delayed by an hour owing to 2 Para's inexperience of embarking in the dark, but all proceeded well after that, with 45 Commando arriving in Ajax Bay opposite the settlement at San Carlos, 40 Commando in four LCUs and four LCVPs landing at Blue Beach One and 2 Para in four LCUs on Blue Beach Two. A further two LCUs proceeded onto the beach and discharged a Scorpion and a Scimitar each of the Blues and Royals, capable of offering fire support. Another contained a combat engineer tractor of the Royal Engineers.

The men disembarked just short of the waterline, completely unopposed, with the troops moving off to dig in on their first objectives while the landing craft came about to collect the second wave. The landings were slightly delayed, but the build-up continued undisturbed, apart from light resistance encountered by 3 Para at Port San Carlos and 45 Commando around Ajax Bay. The only casualties on D-Day occurred when a Sea King escorted by two Gazelles was fired upon by forces on the ground, with both Gazelles downed with the loss of three Royal Marines aircrew. The Argentines began a concerted air attack just before 0900hrs when a Pucará fired on the transport vessel *Canberra*, followed by regular sorties from the mainland and Stanley directed against the escort ships and the landing force. However, most of this effort concentrated on the Navy, leaving the ground forces to continue consolidating unabated, with 2 and 3 Para, and 40 and 45 Commando now ashore and Rapier batteries established on the heights overlooking the inlet to protect shipping from Argentine aircraft. 42 Commando, held in reserve aboard ship during the initial landings, disembarked later in the day.

Royal Marines of 40 Commando man a trench at San Carlos. Much to their frustration, this unit did not take part in the fighting which led to the fall of Stanley, but rather remained behind to defend the initial landing and supply area. (Bridgeman Art Library, PNP 386868)

The merchant ship *Atlantic Conveyor*, which the Argentines sank with an Exocet missile on 25 May. The disaster resulted in the loss of her entire complement of helicopters, apart from one Chinook which was airborne at the time, as well as thousands of tons of stores including ammunition and vital Sea Harrier spare parts. Note the Harrier preparing to land near the bow. (Imperial War Museum, FKD 532)

Events exceeded expectation, though Thompson soon discovered, much to his frustration, that *Canberra*, *Stromness*, *Europic Ferry* and *Norland* were to be withdrawn from San Carlos that evening. These carried between them tens of thousands of rations, tons of ammunition, replacement radio batteries and other vital stores. This left 3 Commando Brigade relying heavily on the logistic support teams to make Herculean efforts to land further supplies than originally planned, barring which the expedition might have found itself safely ashore – yet disastrously undersupplied.

Operation *Sutton* – the landings at San Carlos, had proved a significant achievement: the Task Force had succeeded in landing unopposed the five major units of 3 Commando Brigade and supporting units after more than a month at sea, with a foothold now established in the islands. That said, the Argentines then commenced six days of continuous air attacks, possibly as many as 130 sorties in a dozen or more raids sent from Argentina, against the beachhead and the vessels at San Carlos, soon to be dubbed 'Bomb Alley'. Despite losses like the *Ardent* and *Antelope*, the beachhead remained stable, with over 100,000 tons of supplies landed by the time the air strikes ceased – though they did prevent full disembarkation with implications for supply for the remainder of the conflict.

HAMMER BLOW: GOOSE GREEN, 28 MAY

The day before the landings, Thompson and Lt. Col. 'H' Jones, commander of 2 Para – then holding defensive positions in the Sussex Mountains south of San Carlos Water – considered the possibility of a raid against the closest known Argentine position to the beachhead: Goose Green and the settlement at Darwin. Such an attack would be consistent with Moore's instructions that the troops maintain momentum. Both positions lay only 15 miles (25km) south, but with transport severely limited – only six Sea King 4s and five

Wessex 5s were available for the whole brigade – these aircraft could not accommodate the battalion, which would therefore have to move entirely on foot, for even moving by sea to Brenton Loch under cover of darkness was found, owing to British ignorance of Argentine strength, to be impossible – a conclusion reached by Major Ewan Southby-Tailyour, a Royal Marine who during his pre-war posting in the islands acquired a minutely specialized knowledge of their waters by meticulously charting the coastline in his yacht. Instead, patrols dispatched by 2 Para moved south on 24 May and occupied an empty structure known as Canterra House, 6 miles (10km) from the battalion's position. D Coy was meant to probe even further forward to occupy Camilla Creek House but insufficient numbers of helicopters – a problem to plague British forces hereafter – rendered this impossible.

Political pressure soon mounted for rapid action, for the sinking of the destroyer HMS *Coventry* and the transport vessel *Atlantic Conveyor* by Argentine aircraft on D+4 (25 May) threatened to affect public opinion adversely back home – quite apart from the potentially catastrophic loss suffered of ten helicopters – six Wessexes, three Chinooks and a Lynx – all crucial for the transport of troops and supplies over ground notorious for its lack of roads and the impossibility of most wheeled vehicles to traverse the ubiquitous soft peat. Jones himself was very keen to get moving, and when Thompson received explicit instructions from Northwood to proceed, notwithstanding the lack of transport but with assurances of supporting fire from the Royal Navy, he did not hesitate. The government needed a quick victory and the garrison at Goose Green posed a threat to the newly established base at San Carlos, whose capture would spell disaster to British operations.

Intelligence revealed that the Argentines held the position with at least three companies of infantry, two 105mm howitzers and a large number of anti-aircraft guns, though the SAS, who had carried out a diversionary raid in the area on D-Day wrongly indicated the presence of no more than a single company. In the event, both assessments proved gross underestimates: there were almost exactly 1,000 defenders in the area. If 2 Para had to approach on foot, Jones decided that it must not advance unsupported by artillery and arranged for three 105mm guns to be flown forward at night, with additional firepower to be furnished by the frigate *Arrow*, carrying a 4.5in. gun as her main armament. Jones also planned to make use of two Scout helicopters overhead.

At dusk on 26 May, 2 Para left Sussex Mountain and before first light on the following morning had reached Camilla Creek House and the surrounding area. Two Harriers attacked Goose Green before ground action began, with one aircraft shot down. Around noon Jones was mortified and extremely angered to hear the BBC World Service reporting the presence of a parachute battalion poised to attack Darwin and Goose Green, thereby removing the element of surprise, but he determined that the attack must proceed nonetheless. In the event, the Argentines believed the broadcast a feeble attempt at misinformation and disregarded it.

Jones planned an overcomplicated six-phase assault to be conducted over the night of the 27th and into the following morning. He hoped to limit the numbers of civilian casualties as much as possible by seizing the settlements during the 28th. Three captured Argentines, interrogated by a Spanish-speaking Royal Marine attached to 2 Para, provided some useful intelligence, and further information was gleaned from another Marine who had served on the Falklands and possessed a detailed knowledge of the Darwin–Goose

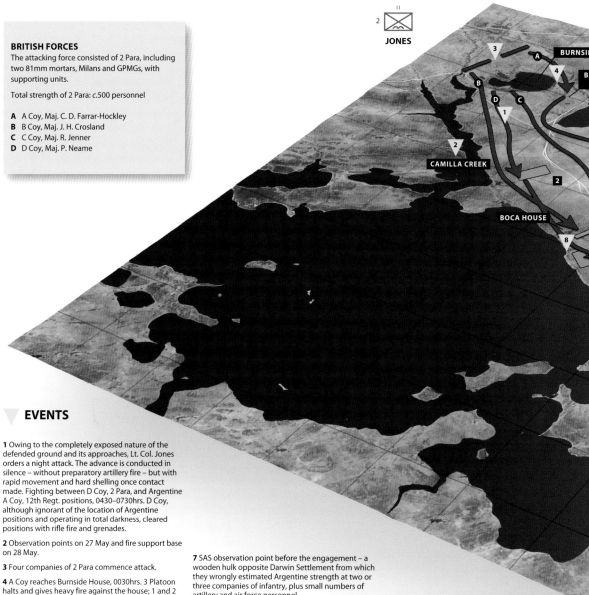

JONES

BURNSIDE

BU H

CAMILLA CREEK

BOCA HOUSE

▼ EVENTS

1 Owing to the completely exposed nature of the defended ground and its approaches, Lt. Col. Jones orders a night attack. The advance is conducted in silence – without preparatory artillery fire – but with rapid movement and hard shelling once contact made. Fighting between D Coy, 2 Para, and Argentine A Coy, 12th Regt. positions, 0430–0730hrs. D Coy, although ignorant of the location of Argentine positions and operating in total darkness, cleared positions with rifle fire and grenades.

2 Observation points on 27 May and fire support base on 28 May.

3 Four companies of 2 Para commence attack.

4 A Coy reaches Burnside House, 0030hrs. 3 Platoon halts and gives heavy fire against the house; 1 and 2 Platoons move around, firing anti-tank rockets at doors and windows and throwing in grenades. In fact, only occupants are four civilians.

5 Although expecting opposition at Coronation Point, A Coy discovers it unoccupied. Farrar-Hockley leaves one platoon here for purposes of acquiring fire support towards the next objective, before carrying on down a track towards Darwin Settlement less than a mile away.

6 Main Argentine defence line. Mixed response from defenders: some offer spirited resistance while others assume the foetal position and cower in their sleeping bags in the bottom of their trenches, there to be shot or captured. British advance halts at Darwin Hill, 0930hrs, with daylight now exposing them to view; Jones, endeavouring to lead a flanking movement to the right of the rise, is killed, 1000hrs, replaced by Maj. Chris Keeble; stalemate until 1300hrs, when trenches rolled up from the extreme left.

7 SAS observation point before the engagement – a wooden hulk opposite Darwin Settlement from which they wrongly estimated Argentine strength at two or three companies of infantry, plus small numbers of artillery and air force personnel.

8 B Coy advance from Start Line at 0400hrs and unknowingly skirt some Argentine positions in the darkness, but their advance is soon blocked by heavy resistance at Boca House. D Coy discovers a narrow path along the shore, outflanks and seizes house, 1230hrs, taking about 20 prisoners while the remaining defenders flee.

9 Argentine company (84 men of the 12th and 25th Regts under Lt. Esteban) arrives after being helicoptered from Stanley, 1230hrs. Poor weather conditions prevent both Harrier ground support to 2 Para as well as air support from the Argentine mainland to the defenders.

10 From the airfield Air Commodore Wilson Pedroza launches three Pucarás and two Aeromacchis against British artillery positions and some Paras, but these inflict little damage, apart from downing a Scout helicopter carrying ammunition forward.

11 Pushing on from Boca House, D Coy approaches the airfield and is attacked by Aeromacchis and Pucarás, of which one each is shot down. The airfield is captured at 1440hrs.

12 C Coy, advancing from Darwin Hill, fights for the schoolhouse and some store buildings, 1500–1600hrs.

13 B Coy cuts off approach to Goose Green Settlement from the south, 1700hrs.

14 B Coy, 12th Regt. arrives from Mt Kent under Cpt. Eduardo Corisiglia, 15 hours after the start of the fighting.

15 Argentine garrison surrenders at Goose Green, 1150hrs; civilians released from Community Centre.

ATTACK BY 2 PARA ON GOOSE GREEN, 28 MAY

The Argentine garrison in the Darwin–Goose Green area posed a potential threat to the British beachhead, while at the same time an early victory would establish early momentum for the ground operations.

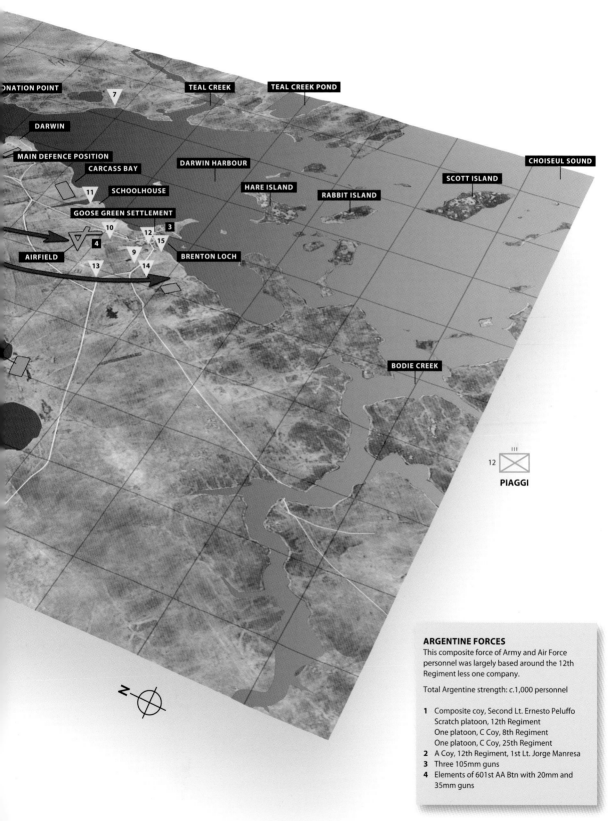

ONATION POINT

TEAL CREEK

TEAL CREEK POND

CHOISEUL SOUND

DARWIN

MAIN DEFENCE POSITION

DARWIN HARBOUR

SCOTT ISLAND

CARCASS BAY

SCHOOLHOUSE

HARE ISLAND

RABBIT ISLAND

GOOSE GREEN SETTLEMENT

AIRFIELD

BRENTON LOCH

BODIE CREEK

12 PIAGGI

ARGENTINE FORCES

This composite force of Army and Air Force personnel was largely based around the 12th Regiment less one company.

Total Argentine strength: c.1,000 personnel

1 Composite coy, Second Lt. Ernesto Peluffo
   Scratch platoon, 12th Regiment
   One platoon, C Coy, 8th Regiment
   One platoon, C Coy, 25th Regiment
2 A Coy, 12th Regiment, 1st Lt. Jorge Manresa
3 Three 105mm guns
4 Elements of 601st AA Btn with 20mm and
   35mm guns

Green area. Meanwhile, 2 Para remained undetected for most of the 27th around Camilla Creek House, sending out probing patrols which brought back intelligence on Argentine positions.

Jones held an Orders Group, inspected recent air-reconnaissance photographs and reviewed the position of Argentine minefields indicated on a captured map. His line of approach was necessarily limited owing to the geographical confines of the narrow isthmus on which his objectives stood, with Burntside House just ahead of the battalion's start line. This confined Jones, who lacked air transport, to a direct north–south approach, with little apparent opportunity for a flank attack against an easily defensible position held by the 12th Regiment. While 2 Para prepared its plan of assault, 3 Para and 45 Commando were moving to the north and east of East Falkland.

At 0230hrs on the 28th, A Coy advanced on the left flank and made contact with the first of the Argentine troops in that sector, driving them off 20 minutes later. B Coy, attacking on the right flank, encountered strongly held positions. Lieutenant Clive Chapman, 6 Platoon recalled how:

> Just about every trench encountered was grenaded.... There was a continuous momentum throughout the attack and it was very swiftly executed. The Argentinian resistance was pretty weak. A lot of them were, I believe, trying to hide in the bottom of their trenches and ignore the fight. They were a scared bunch, and a lot of them were non-participants.
>
> The success of the attack had an electrifying impact on the platoon. I think we believed from there on in that we were invincible. I am a great believer in the force of 'will' in battle, and the fact that we had imposed our will so well and so early, made us a better platoon.

The first objectives were not, however, taken until about 0400hrs, including A Coy in possession of Coronation Point and D Coy holding the centre position. Simultaneously, *Arrow* offered fire support managed by the Forward Observation Officer (FOO) until sunrise. At first light, A Coy moved off again and encountered heavy resistance from machine-gun fire, forcing it to halt while B Coy was held up by the strongpoint of Boca House, with no effective weapons available to neutralize it. Jones and his Tac HQ moved up to determine the cause of the delay, much of it caused by the difficulties encountered in dislodging the defenders from their trenches and bunkers. Immensely frustrated by the slow progress, Jones raced ahead and charged a machine-gun position on his own, receiving a mortal wound but inspiring A Coy, commanded by Major Dair Farrar-Hockley, to surge forwards. Meanwhile, the two Scout helicopters continued to ferry ammunition forward and evacuate casualties to the rear, including the battalion's fallen commander, though a Pucará shot down one of these aircraft.

The loss of Jones could not be allowed to hold up the offensive, and Major Chris Keeble, the second in command, arrived rapidly by helicopter from the battalion's main HQ to assume command. B and D Companies continued to engage the Argentines to the west of Goose Green meeting strong opposition, though Major John Crosland, OC B Coy understood how to break the deadlock at Boca House – by bringing up the Milan team:

> A Milan is an anti-tank weapon, which fires a guided missile with a very substantial warhead over a range of 2,000 metres. I thought, if we can bust them with the Milans, we can probably get round their flank, get down to Darwin, knock that off and then worry about Goose Green. The Milan was an unorthodox choice, but it was the only powerful weapon we had. Much to our relief, the first round fired was a perfect bull's eye. It went straight through the bunker window and blew it out completely, and the second one did the same. Four more rounds and that was Boca House cleared out. Everyone stood on their feet and cheered!

This helped turn the Argentine left flank and while C Coy assumed A Coy's position in the centre, D Coy captured the airstrip and B Coy engaged a company of Argentine reinforcements arrived by air from Mt Kent. All the while, Skyhawks hampered the British advance until around 1525hrs when the arrival of two Harriers obliged them to cease their attacks. By sunset 2 Para had taken Darwin and surrounded the Goose Green settlement, though they had to remain exposed to freezing conditions throughout the night, in the course of which helicopters evacuated the wounded lest they die from exposure. At dawn on the 29th Keeble sent two Argentine prisoners into Goose Green with an ultimatum and terms for the garrison's surrender. At 1450hrs the garrison commander agreed to the terms. It was a remarkable achievement, with 2 Para triumphant against odds of more than two to one. None of the 112 civilians in the area had been harmed, though 2 Para lost 16 men killed and 36 severely wounded, plus another c.30 suffering from minor injuries. A Royal Engineer and Royal Marine pilot were also killed. The Argentines lost 45 men killed, 90 wounded and 961 captured, mostly from the 25th Infantry Regiment.

PREPARATIONS AND APPROACH TO STANLEY

While British forces were engaged at Goose Green, a major advance was under way to the north, prompted by orders to Brig. Thompson to leave the beachhead and establish an investment of Stanley amongst the rocky features immediately to the west of the town. The bulk of the brigade was meant to proceed north of the ridge of high ground that stretched across most of East

LIEUTENANT-COLONEL 'H' JONES MORTALLY WOUNDED DURING THE ASSAULT ON DARWIN–GOOSE GREEN (pp. 44–45)

In his plan of attack Lt. Col. 'H' Jones did not envisage his appearance directly in the front line. Indeed, the role of a unit commander demands that he remain well back, in touch with all company commanders via the battalion net and thereby able both to stay abreast of progress and to issue orders accordingly. Personally intervening out of frustration at learning that A Company's attack had faltered on Darwin Hill, Jones (1) and his Tac HQ (2) – the latter actually outpaced by Jones at the time he was shot – charged up a re-entrant in an attempt to outflank the defenders dug-in on the crest, where the colonel received a mortal wound inflicted by a single bullet entering just behind his right collarbone. While Jones's bravery is incontestable – he received a posthumous VC – the wisdom of his conduct has remained contentious ever since.

Critics of Jones's conduct assert that when he assembled his Orders Group, consisting of his company commanders, to brief them on details of the mission he pressurized his intelligence officer to provide grid references at a rapid pace, compounding the confusion already created by his complex six-phase plan of attack, which included precise timings to which Jones unrealistically expected his company commanders to adhere. The O Group became a rushed, tense affair out of which the true positions held by the defenders remained unclear. By imposing restrictive control on his company commanders Jones did not account for the Argentine response; failed adequately to explain 2 Para's mission; formulated his plan based on faulty intelligence of both the defenders' strength and dispositions; denied his subordinates the ability to use their innate intelligence to achieve their commander's objective as they saw fit rather than adhering to Jones's overly complex set of instructions – that is, applying the principle of Mission Command, whereby a commander states his intent but does not dictate in precise terms the manner in which the object is to be achieved, and thus permitting subordinate officers to exercise their initiative according to changing circumstances in the field.

Supporters of Jones's conduct argue that his action reflected the bold, aggressive ethos of the Parachute Regiment and the colonel's view that early victory was essential for setting the right tone for operations to follow; that he could not be blamed for faulty SAS reconnaissance, which erroneously judged Argentine morale and strength as low and their defences to be poorly organized; that his unit had not served in action under its newly appointed commander; that his presence on the spot restored the momentum of a stalled attack conducted over open ground in full daylight; and that his swift, decisive action not only served as a conspicuous example of bravery but fulfilled an officer's responsibility to lead from the front. In short, having assessed the situation and appreciating that only a fleeting opportunity to act decisively existed, Jones seized the initiative and broke the impasse – selflessly sacrificing himself for the sake of the mission's success – and a spectacular one at that.

Falkland, a move intended to be conducted by helicopter; but with the loss of the *Atlantic Conveyor* most of Thompson's brigade were obliged to move on foot, with Teal Inlet as their first objective, 25 miles (40km) from San Carlos. Another 20 miles (32km) would then separate them from the Argentine positions around Stanley, but reconnaissance by an SBS team, inserted earlier by small boat and helicopter, revealed that no Argentine forces were present in the Teal area. Nevertheless, Thompson remained aware that Pucará aircraft might still pose a danger on the line of march, and that deteriorating weather conditions threatened to slow the advance.

Thompson's plan called for 45 Commando marching to Teal Inlet via the settlement at Douglas, making use of a rudimentary track for most of the route. Originally, 3 Para, 460 all ranks, were to follow them until they reached Douglas, where the infantry would then take the lead as far as Teal. But, owing to the rivalry between the units, 3 Para discussed an alternative route with an islander and discovered a more direct route to Teal which obviated the need of moving via Douglas – albeit without the benefit of a track.

In a trek marked by immense endurance and eye-watering exhaustion, both units left the beachhead on 27 May, the Marines moving first by landing craft from Ajax Bay to Port San Carlos. 45 Commando then proceeded to 'yomp' – the Royal Marines' term for a long, loaded march – for 13 hours, covering 14 miles (23km) over very treacherous surfaces, in the course of which 15 men left the ranks through fatigue or injury, to be recovered later by Scout helicopter or cross-country vehicles. The boggy peat, broken by slippery rock and uneven, pitted ground rendered the advance exceedingly tough to negotiate, for the troops moved in total darkness with between 100 and 130lb (45–60kg), depending on the gear they carried. Those burdened with anti-armour weapons or heavy ordnance were forced to dig deep into their physical and mental reserves to meet this particularly gargantuan effort. Captain Ian Gardiner, commander of X Coy, 45 Commando, described the dreadful ordeal thus:

LEFT
A Marine of 45 Commando resting in Stanley at the conclusion of the 25-day ground campaign on East Falkland. These extraordinary fighting men proved more than a match for the demoralized and badly led Argentine garrison. (Imperial War Museum, FKD 157)

RIGHT
Men of 5 Infantry Brigade silhouetted at dusk during the landings at San Carlos on 2 June. The principal units consisted of 1/7 Gurkhas, 2 Scots Guards and 1 Welsh Guards. (Imperial War Museum, FKD 349)

Royal Marines of 45 Commando cross a muddy field after leaving Teal Inlet on the last leg of their 'yomp' to the mountains near Stanley. (Imperial War Museum, FKD 2270)

The walk from Port San Carlos to New House, some 20km, was the worst of my life. The weather was not too bad but the ground was boggy. Where it was not boggy, there were strong lumps and tufts of grass which, however one stands on them, even in daylight, one stands a good chance of turning one's ankle. In places it was pretty steep but all faded into insignificance compared to the cursed weight we were carrying – much of which I knew to be wholly unnecessary. I probably made things worse for myself by allowing my bitterness to burn up energy – but the marines were magnificent. We lost the first man after 200 yards – a man known to be the Company skate [heavy drinker] – and about six more over the next few hours. They were mostly the weaker-spirited men who, although they possibly did have something wrong with them, would probably have found some pretext or other to roll around in agony in any event. The rest went on with the greatest of stoicism and good humour all day and through until 2 o'clock the following morning. I was immensely proud of them. If possible, marching in darkness was worse than daylight, and, for those at the tail end of a queue of 600 men bumping and stumbling through the black night, life must have been hell. I was fairly pre-occupied by trying to keep people together and perhaps didn't notice so much, but by the time we leaguered up, I was near my wit's end.

The Marines did not bed down until 0200hrs, their sleeping bags soaking, but relieved to unburden themselves of their Bergens. Later that morning they proceeded to Douglas Settlement to the enthusiastic welcome of its 22 residents.

3 Para, meanwhile, had a shorter distance to cover with slightly lighter haversacks and 'tabbed' (derived from the Army term 'tab', short for 'tactical advance to battle') their way to Teal, which they accomplished in two parts, moving across 20 miles (32km) of ground – without the benefit of marked tracks – in 33 hours and sleeping exposed to the cold without the benefit of sleeping bags. A tank troop of the Blues and Royals accompanied both units and proceeded without incident despite predictions that the weight of their tanks would leave them stuck in the soft peat. So long as they did not alter course and unduly disturb the softest part of the ground, these vehicles could both remain in motion and clear the way for others behind.

British advance on Stanley, 27 May to 8 June

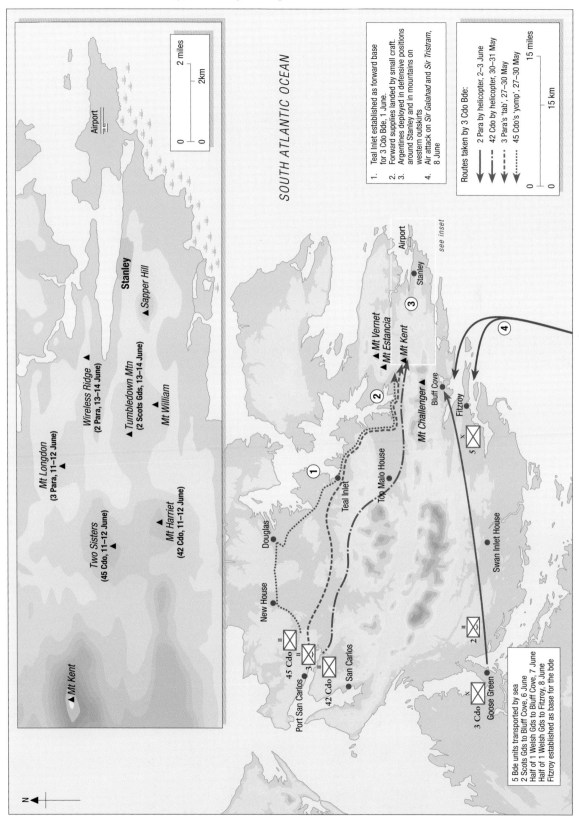

SOUTH ATLANTIC OCEAN

1. Teal Inlet established as forward base for 3 Cdo Bde, 1 June.
2. Forward supplies landed by small craft.
3. Argentines deployed in defensive positions around Stanley and in mountains on western outskirts.
4. Air attack on *Sir Galahad* and *Sir Tristram*, 8 June.

Routes taken by 3 Cdo Bde:
— 2 Para by helicopter, 2–3 June
—·— 42 Cdo by helicopter, 30–31 May
—--— 3 Para's 'tab', 27–30 May
······ 45 Cdo's 'yomp', 27–30 May

0   15 miles
0   15 km

Airport
Stanley

see inset

▲ Mt Vernet
▲ Mt Estancia
▲ Mt Kent

3

2

Mt Challenger ▲
Bluff Cove ●

Fitzroy ●
x
5

Top Malo House

1

Teal Inlet ●

Douglas ●

New House ●

4

Swan Inlet House ●

x
2

45 Cdo
3
Port San Carlos ●

42 Cdo
● San Carlos

3 Cdo
x
● Goose Green

5 Bde units transported by sea
2 Scots Gds to Bluff Cove, 6 June
Half of 1 Welsh Gds to Bluff Cove, 7 June
Half of 1 Welsh Gds to Fitzroy, 8 June
Fitzroy established as base for the bde

N

0   2 miles
0   2km

Airport

Stanley

▲ Sapper Hill

Wireless Ridge ▲
(2 Para, 13–14 June)

▲ Tumbledown Mtn
(2 Scots Gds, 13–14 June)

Mt William ▲

Mt Longdon ▲
(3 Para, 11–12 June)

Two Sisters ▲
(45 Cdo, 11–12 June)

Mt Harriet ▲
(42 Cdo, 11–12 June)

▲ Mt Kent

49

3 Para, exhausted after its epic march, reached the outskirts of Teal Inlet, a tiny settlement of a handful of houses, on the night of 28 May, but located only one Argentine soldier present. 45 Commando, similarly fatigued with many men suffering from trench foot, arrived on the night of the 30th.

Meanwhile, on the 29th, action took place on Mt Kent, a 1,500ft-high (450m) eminence – the largest of the hills around Stanley and only 12 miles (19km) from the port. With action at Goose Green complete, Thompson released his two helicopters and some of his troops to assault Mt Kent, which SAS reconnaissance reported as weakly defended. The assault would be carried out at night, with 42 Commando brought forward by Sea Kings and Chinooks with half a battery of guns. The capture of Mt Kent offered a number of advantages: it lay 16 miles (26km) closer to Stanley than Teal Inlet and, being the tallest of the features west of the capital, overlooked all the main Argentine defences, which stood on a series of heights of varying elevation: Mt Harriet, Two Sisters, Mt Longdon, Mt Tumbledown, Mt William, Wireless Ridge and Sapper Hill. In the event, circumstances would oblige the British to contest possession of six of these positions.

The operation began on the evening of 29–30 May. Part of K Coy, 42 Commando, went aboard three Sea Kings and proceeded in the direction of Mt Kent, 40 miles (64km) away, but was forced to return owing to snowstorms. The following night the helicopters tried again, this time with greater success. Three flights by the three Sea Kings transported K Coy, Tactical HQ, four heavy mortar teams and a Blowpipe detachment, together with three 105mm guns and their 22-man crew. The troops landed near the base of Mt Kent; K Coy proceeded to the mountain and discovered it unoccupied, for Menéndez had sent a company of 12th Regiment to reinforce the rest of its parent unit at Goose Green, and thus could not spare enough forces to hold both Mt Kent and Two Sisters. As a consequence, apart from a patrol driven off by the SAS, Mt Kent was deserted. In fact, the Argentine positions formed an arc covering Mt Longdon, Two Sisters and Mt Harriet.

Heavily laden British soldiers wait to embark by helicopter. (Imperial War Museum, FKD 2124)

Argentine soldiers in an underground dugout. Respectable defences like these dotted the elevated features immediately west of Stanley, but in general the defenders' fieldcraft left much to be desired. (Imperial War Museum, FKD 2446)

The arrival of troops, however small in number, at Mt Kent, represented a significant achievement, for it was performed with a minimum of helicopter support and enabled the placement of guns within range of Argentine defenders in the area around Moody Brook, 10 miles (16km) away. In fact, the guns could just about reach the outskirts of Stanley itself.

Thompson now decided to move 3 Para and 42 Commando forwards towards the outskirts of Stanley, but without if possible provoking a major engagement, for 3 Commando Brigade lacked both support and supplies. A patrol sighted Argentine helicopters landing 17 men at Top Malo House, a remote, unoccupied shepherd's house. Nineteen men from the Royal Marines' specialized training unit, the Mountain and Arctic Warfare Cadre, travelling by Sea King the following morning and flying just above the ground, landed near their target and engaged the Argentines, killing five and taking 12 prisoners, of whom seven were injured. The Argentines had put up a spirited resistance, with their commander receiving four wounds before surrendering. Three Royal Marines were wounded. The following day, 14 Argentines posted on Mt Simon and Malo Hill, from where they had witnessed the fight, came forwards to surrender to 3 Para.

As the weather worsened 3 Para continued its advance, guided by an islander, and reached Estancia House, an isolated structure occupied by local civilians who provided tea and food to the exhausted troops. From there 3 Para discovered that there were no Argentine defenders on either Mt Estancia or Mt Vernet, upon which the Paras occupied these points. As a result of these movements 3 Para and 42 Commando controlled a chain of peaks 7 miles (11km) in length, with the Argentine positions to their front, separated by unoccupied ground ranging in width from 2 miles (3km) in the south to 5 miles (8km) in the north. Still, the troops could at present advance no further, for 3 Commando Brigade had reached the extent of its supply line, which now stretched tenuously back to San Carlos. Two of Thompson's units stood on high ground as the weather began to turn bad, with the first snow falling on 1 June. Teal Inlet became the forward base, but demands for helicopters elsewhere prevented the rapid build-up of supplies demanded.

Some supply ships could sail as far as Teal, situated 12 miles (19km) inland from the entrance of Port Salvador, while the crew of the *Intrepid* created ad hoc minesweepers out of small landing craft to clear the way. Once the area was discovered to be free of mines the entrance was opened and supplies began to flow the following night when *Sir Percival* brought the first run from San Carlos. She and *Sir Geraint* continued the build-up of stores at Teal, making possible the engagements which were soon to follow.

Recent events marked a notable point of success for the British for, by establishing a forward base at Teal, which also became Thompson's headquarters, three battalions had arrived on the outskirts of Stanley almost entirely on foot, representing a movement of three-quarters the distance of East Falkland, positioning them just beyond contact with the main Argentine defences. This the Marines and Paras had accomplished with relatively little support from vehicles or helicopters – a testament to their determination and high standard of fitness. Most impressive of all, the brigade had achieved this feat within a week of Thompson receiving orders to move out from the San Carlos beachhead.

On 30 May, Maj. Gen. Jeremy Moore and Brig. Tony Wilson arrived at San Carlos aboard HMS *Fearless*, having travelled down on the *QE2*, then moored safely at South Georgia. From San Carlos, Moore held the position of Commander Land Forces Falkland Islands, while Wilson waited for the arrival of his 5 Infantry Brigade, consisting of 1/7 Gurkha Rifles, 1 Welsh Guards, 2 Scots Guards and supporting arms from the Royal Artillery, Royal Engineers, Royal Signals, REME, RAMC and other corps. With Moore's appearance Thompson passed to him control over all land forces. After a rapid shift of command, Thompson shifted the headquarters of 3 Commando Brigade to Teal Inlet, which allowed him to transfer close to his troops.

Moore, for his part, found himself assuming command under very favourable circumstances. The British controlled a secure base at San Carlos and 2 Para had achieved remarkable success at Goose Green. Moore soon reorganized his troops: 2 Para and 29 Battery, which had been detached from 5 Infantry Brigade before sailing to the South Atlantic as part of 3 Commando Brigade, reverted to 5 Infantry Brigade command. 40 Commando received orders to remain at San Carlos to defend that base. 5 Infantry Brigade was to be dispatched east on the southern flank facing the Stanley defences. The Gurkhas of 5 Infantry Brigade were the first to be given a mission. Most of the battalion was flown by Chinook to Goose Green where they replaced 2 Para and began to patrol the area, sometimes on foot, other times with civilian tractors and trailers or with helicopters, taking in the course of this effort ten prisoners, most at Egg Harbour House, 18 miles (29km) from Goose Green off Falkland Sound. A search by helicopter for other Argentines on Lafonia produced no further prisoners. By being the first unit from 5 Infantry Brigade to be deployed, the Gurkhas operated under the illusion that they might be the first to be in action; in fact, their assignment to the Goose Green area relegated them to being the last unit in the brigade to be sent east, which denied them a part in the final battles, narrowly missing the chance to come to grips with the Argentines on Mt William.

Moore's position at the beginning of June therefore stood thus: 3 Commando Brigade had three of its battalions in place on the northern flank, but with the loss of the three Chinooks aboard *Atlantic Conveyor* on 25 May, he was denied the lift capacity to transport 5 Infantry Brigade to the southern flank while simultaneously maintaining adequate levels of supplies and food

for 3 Commando Brigade's forward units. Wilson therefore decided that the best option was to march his brigade down the track south of the mountains west of Stanley. This posed a number of difficulties, the principal one being that no settlements or usable harbours stood along the proposed route, thus denying the troops the ability to rest or receive supplies on the 35-mile (56km) line of march from Goose Green to Fitzroy Settlement. It was also unclear whether the two Guards battalions possessed the stamina to undertake such an arduous march, as they were accustomed to movement by lorry and followed a much less strenuous training regime than the Paras and Marines.

A rapid decision and fortunate circumstances solved the problem. On the afternoon of 2 June, Maj. Chris Keeble, acting commander of 2 Para in the wake of Jones's death, proposed that a small group move by helicopter to Swan Inlet House – a point approximately midway between Goose Green and Fitzroy. The house was thought to be empty; if the telephone line to Fitzroy remained intact it might be possible to call residents at Fitzroy to determine the strength of any Argentine garrison present. Five Scout helicopters from 656 Squadron were fortunately available to 5 Infantry Brigade at Goose Green, together with a Chinook on hand for the day for purposes of moving stores around San Carlos and to Goose Green. A plan was drawn up rapidly: the Scout helicopters would move a small number of Paras to Swan Inlet House and seek to telephone Fitzroy in the hope of learning if any Argentines were present there. If not, 2 Para could begin its move by means of the Chinook and the Scouts. Accordingly, these flew through light mist along the coast, less than 50ft (15m) above the water, encountering no opposition in flight and discovering Swan Inlet House abandoned. Major John Crosland of 2 Para made telephone contact with a resident who related that the small numbers of Argentines recently at Fitzroy and at the nearby Bluff Cove Settlement had since left. With the way now clear to move 5 Infantry Brigade, the helicopters returned the Paras to Goose Green in an operation lasting less than an hour.

Back at Goose Green helicopters were rapidly loaded and dispatched. The Chinook conveyed over 50 Paras, and the Scout pilots, by stripping out their machine guns, could now transport four Paras. In all, the helicopters flew several sorties, refuelling from abandoned Argentine fuel drums, and deposited the bulk of two companies and 2 Para's headquarters to Fitzroy and Bluff Cove, 3 miles (5km) away, before dark. There was considerable risk attached to Wilson's decision to commit the bulk of his brigade so far forward, for it now lacked support or a source of supply. 2 Para, still

LEFT
An Argentine Air Force C-130 Hercules transport aircraft on the runway at Stanley airfield. These mammoth machines played an important role in moving troops and supplies in and out of the Falklands. Once the ground campaign began, inbound aircraft carrying supplies returned to the mainland with Argentine wounded. (Imperial War Museum, FKD 2181)

RIGHT
Residents of Stanley carry on with their daily routine as Argentine armoured personnel carriers of the Amphibious Vehicle Battalion line a road in Port Stanley. Only three Falkland Islanders lost their lives – to a Royal Artillery shell accidentally fired into the town. (Imperial War Museum, FKD 2174)

recovering from its action at Goose Green, stood particularly vulnerable at this time, and might have experienced grave difficulty in the event of an Argentine strike to the south. The Paras had no artillery, no defence against air attack and no support from other infantry to hand.

Nevertheless, on the following day, 3 June, Sea Kings moved the rest of the battalion forward, but, with insufficient numbers of helicopters available to shift any other substantial unit, Wilson decided that the remainder of 5 Infantry Brigade and its air defences would be transported in components by sea, under cover of darkness. The assault ships HMS *Fearless* and *Intrepid* were to be sent, on separate nights to lessen the risk if aircraft attacked, conveying troops half the way to Bluff Cove before transferring the men to landing craft for the rest of the way. As planned, on the night of 5–6 June the first journey took place, *Intrepid* leaving at dusk with the Scots Guards aboard and transferring them later to landing craft, which brought them safely to Bluff Cove.

On the evening of 6–7 June *Fearless* set off with the Welsh Guards, but owing to a misunderstanding over the manner of transferring them by landing craft from a point halfway to Bluff Cove, left only half the battalion at their destination and returned with the remainder to San Carlos. The remaining Guardsmen then transferred to the *Sir Galahad* along with Rapiers and stores, for, unlike *Intrepid*, *Galahad* was already bound for Fitzroy, so Bluff Cove constituted only a short extension to the journey. The *Sir Galahad* sailed late on the 7th and reached Fitzroy about 0800hrs on the following morning. Following a series of unfortunate events the Welsh Guards were still aboard when five Skyhawks attacked the *Sir Galahad* and *Sir Tristram* near Fitzroy killing only two crewmen aboard the latter, but dropping three bombs on *Sir Galahad*, aboard which an inferno erupted when fires ignited tons of ammunition and fuel causing an explosion that killed 48 men and injured or burned another 115 – a tragedy that excluded the Welsh Guards from major operations thereafter, for they met only slight resistance at Sapper Hill early on 14 June, when with 40 Commando they helicoptered in and drove off a small force.

THE FINAL OFFENSIVE

The climax of the campaign on land consisted of a series of engagements fought in the hills just west of Stanley; but before describing these it is instructive to consider the Argentine position.

Notwithstanding the defeat at Goose Green, Menéndez's command still consisted of 11,000 troops, which remained numerically superior to the British. On the other hand, 2,000 of these, consisting of two infantry regiments and supporting troops, may be discounted for, in their position at Port Howard and Fox Bay on West Falkland, these forces found themselves isolated and unable to take part in operations elsewhere. Meanwhile, around Stanley, approximately 8,500 to 9,000 troops comprised the garrison, but of these fewer than 5,500 consisted of infantry. Their quality varied, with the majority conscripts, though well emplaced and more numerous than their attackers. Menéndez had originally disposed his troops on the basis of two assumptions: first, that Britain and Argentina might reach a diplomatic compromise before the Task Force arrived or, in any event, before a major confrontation took place; and second, that if negotiations failed and a landing did occur, it would take place near Stanley, which must inevitably stand as the main objective. The Argentines had wrongly calculated that a landing at or in the vicinity of Stanley under cover of a naval bombardment and carrier-borne aircraft, even if launched against a defended beach, stood a better chance of success than a long trek across difficult, trackless ground via a distant landing site – hence their concentration around the capital. It was, after all, by direct routes that the Argentines had themselves captured Stanley on 2 April, and since Menéndez assumed that the British would adopt the same method to retake the town, he naturally retained his best troops in that sector.

This course amounted to a serious miscalculation. When the British landed at San Carlos, Menéndez was not in a position to oppose them or even make any meaningful move against either the beachhead or the subsequent advance. Galtieri declined Menéndez's request for a thrust against San Carlos direct from the Argentine mainland, which the government regarded as too hazardous and, indeed, unnecessary given the strength of Argentine forces already in the Falklands. Still, notwithstanding his precarious position, Menéndez had not been remiss in preparing his defences around Stanley, for his troops occupied sangars and gun positions, and protected a number of their positions with extensive minefields. Yet the defenders were poorly placed, for most of the troops were deployed and the defences situated to oppose a landing either on the peninsula on which sat the airport east of Stanley or on the beaches to the south. Even when it was clear that the British approach was through the mountains to the west, Menéndez continued to regard the possibility of an enemy landing near Stanley as viable, as a result of which he made only one modification to his plan of defence. From its position facing south on Mt Challenger, Wall Mountain and Mt Harriet, the 4th Regiment was shifted north, leaving Challenger and Wall undefended, and remaining *in situ* on Mt Harriet and occupying Two Sisters. At the same time the Argentines sowed more mines, some indiscriminately by helicopter.

In the meantime, while the Argentines could not resupply themselves, they had managed to bring in stocks by disregarding the potential British submarine threat – which in the event was not sufficient to disrupt supply lines. Thus, a large quantity of *matériel* arrived by sea in the month between the arrival of the Argentine invasion force and the appearance of the Task Force in early May. In fact, along the waterfront at Stanley stood numerous containers of food and clothing – even wine and cigarettes – yet the distribution system operated poorly, with much of the stockpiles sitting idle while many units beyond the capital's limits were forced to cope with locally held, usually meagre, supplies. The stockpiles may have represented Menéndez's efforts to withstand an anticipated siege, but notwithstanding this precaution, his distribution system failed at the rudimentary level. When those units assigned to defensive positions beyond Stanley arrived in the islands, the vast array of support vehicles that landed with them were incapable of negotiating the ground apart from the local tracks which extended short distances beyond the town, leaving open areas – where much of the infantry established their positions – beyond their reach. Shortages of supplies need not have occurred for this reason alone; but the Argentines failed to deploy sufficient numbers of helicopters and this, combined with the serious losses inflicted by the RAF, left many infantry units out in the field with little to eat. The Harriers in particular had wreaked a heavy toll, which persuaded the Argentines to withdraw the last two Chinooks to the mainland on 8 June.

The rapid deployment of reinforcements from Argentina meant that some units arrived without their cooking equipment and could not prepare hot food without depending on the assistance of other units in the area. Severe shortages of meat and bread – basic staples for the Argentines – badly affected morale and led the Stanley garrison to slaughter every sheep in the area, with recourse then taken to killing the local herd of dairy cows. In mid-May, Harriers had exacerbated an already frustrating situation by disabling one of the key Argentine supply ships in Fox Bay, forcing her to abandon much of her load of flour, although small boats later recovered part of this consignment. Approximately two tons of supplies continued to reach the troops by nightly air transport until the very end of the campaign, but this proved woefully inadequate. Aircraft returning to the mainland on such flights evacuated the Argentine wounded from Stanley, thus relieving that burden from the garrison, but stocks of artillery shells never reached sufficient levels even while small-arms ammunition existed in abundance. Circumstances became so severe that small groups of Argentine soldiers, with not inconsiderable amounts of money, would solicit civilians to buy – usually without success – food for them at local shops, where they were banned by order of Menéndez.

Argentine morale suffered not merely from inadequate rations and poor relations between officers and other ranks; the troops disliked the bleak, cold and inhospitable nature of the land, with many Argentines hailing from considerably warmer climes, while the islanders themselves patently rejected the Argentine claim of 'liberation', thus undermining some soldiers' faith in the justice of their cause. Other factors contributed to the low state of morale. While units were meant to return home to be exchanged by rotating mainland formations, this did not come to pass. Propaganda from Buenos Aires about success against the British soon revealed itself to be short of the truth: it was apparent the offensive had not even been blunted, much less repulsed, with the enemy's proximity to Stanley tangible proof of this. The breakdown in discipline manifested itself in a number of ways, such as hungry troops pilfering from the islanders' gardens and chicken-coops or simply begging for food.

Moore had originally planned to attack the defences around Stanley on the evening of 8–9 June, but shortages of supplies – in particular lack of sufficient artillery shells close to the front line – delayed action by two nights. A further postponement of 24 hours occurred when the crippling of the *Sir Galahad* interfered with the helicopter schedules, although other helicopters arrived via the *Engadine* on 9 June. These circumstances thus delayed the movement of British troops in forward areas by four days and nights in adverse conditions – specifically, 3 Para, 45 Commando and 42 Commando, all situated in the areas around Mounts Vernet, Kent and Challenger, with the Scots Guards from 5 Infantry Brigade beyond Bluff Cove. The British had to attack imminently before the conditions these troops were experiencing sapped their strength, damaged their health and consequently affected operational effectiveness. Exposure had yet to take a significant toll, but this was now only a matter of time.

Marine Nigel Rees, of 42 Commando, described the severe conditions, which included biting wind, sleet and snow:

> It boiled down to personal survival. I was very cold; sometimes we were in the clouds. The wind was horrific, always whipping across the top of that mountain. We could not dig in; we only had makeshift bivvies [bivouacs]. The main problem was staying dry. We tried desperately to keep our feet dry. The feet are your main thing; it doesn't matter what happens to the rest of you. We had Cairngorm boots which were very good but, when wet, they retained the water and became thick and heavy and got very cold. You would take your boots off, then the socks off, put the wet socks inside your shirt next to the body and try to dry them out while you were asleep. While you were asleep, you kept your feet dry in your sleeping bag – if that wasn't wet; if it was wet – tough. Then, in the morning, you put your spare socks on and your wet boots back on, and were ready for another day.
>
> For rations we had to go back down the mountain to the helicopter landing zone and carry the rations up in boxes. It was only a kilometre's yomp but it developed into a right pain in the you-know-what. That kilometre took up to two hours to do over rock screes and steep ground. One party lost its way in the fog and took four hours.

Further delays could compromise success, particularly when heavy seas threatened to imperil supply lines. The Argentines were scarcely better off in terms of the effects of deteriorating climate, but their conditions stood marginally better, with shelter established in prepared positions and Stanley behind them, whereas British troops were now well east of San Carlos.

Throughout this period, as the troops waited for orders to advance, reconnaissance went on apace every evening, during which time patrols, often without any casualties sustained, brought in important intelligence about Argentine positions. Nonetheless, patrols occasionally encountered minefields, with consequent losses to a small number of personnel who generally suffered injury rather than death, though in at least one 'blue-on-blue' incident, Marines killed four of their own and wounded three others. Reconnaissance conducted by the Royal Marines went in tandem with covert operations carried out by the SAS and SBS, notably the latter's penetration of Stanley Harbour, where a group hid in the hulk of an old wreck, the *Lady Elizabeth*, in Whalebone Cove. From their position, the SBS could observe the waterfront at 2 miles' (3km) distance and report on troop movements and flights. Over on West Falkland, the SAS continued their operations. When 5th Regiment spotted an SAS observation post near Port Howard it engaged it, killing one trooper but failing to prevent the escape of a second.

All the while, the logistical support continued with remarkable efficiency, and without which the ground forces simply could not operate. Troops poised for an attack on the Stanley defences depended upon a supply chain which extended not simply to Teal Inlet, Fitzroy or San Carlos, but stretched on to Ascension Island and all the way back to Britain. This whole chain depended upon thousands, including helicopter crew, the personnel of the Royal Logistic Corps tasked with moving supplies to forward areas, the crews of the supply ships, the crews of the Hercules transports flying 16-hour long-haul flights to and from Ascension carrying supplies, the tanker crews at Ascension and the transport squadrons of the Royal Air Force, which flew regular sorties from bases at Lyneham and Brize Norton with essential supplies from Britain. This highlights the degree to which Britain had by this time achieved naval superiority and could maintain a secure air bridge even at a distance of 8,000 miles (13,000km), to the extent that while Argentine forces only 400 miles (650km) from the mainland suffered from shortages in food and artillery shells, British forces on the outskirts of Stanley found themselves adequately supplied, albeit with problems regarding protection from the climate, particularly boots not fit for purpose.

Moore, having shifted his headquarters from San Carlos to Fitzroy, had laid plans for the coming offensive – the largest of its kind since World War II. For this task he had available the equivalent of seven battalions of infantry: 42 and 45 Commandos, 2 and 3 Para, 1 Welsh Guards (supplemented by two companies of 40 Commando to compensate for losses on the *Sir Galahad*), 2 Scots Guards and 1/7 Gurkhas (minus one company detached at Goose Green). In support, the artillery supplied 30 105mm guns from 7, 8 and 79 Batteries of 29 Commando Regiment and 29 and 97 Batteries of 4 Field Regiment. There was also limited armoured support in the form of eight light tanks of the Blues and Royals, but the rough and steep terrain rendered them of limited use against some of the elevated Argentine positions.

Major-General Moore had two strategic options: advancing on a broad front or on a narrow one. A narrow thrust through the south, which would avoid confrontation with the Argentine positions in the north, would necessitate the capture of Mt Harriet and Two Sisters by one brigade, followed by Tumbledown Mountain and Mt William by the other. This would then leave only the less formidable obstacle of Sapper Hill before Stanley itself. This plan would obviate the need to engage the Argentines in potentially expensive operations against Mt Longdon and Wireless Ridge. Moreover, the plan suited the circumstances of limited supply of artillery ammunition, with shells required only against a few objectives instead of a broad range. However, after careful thought and in consultation with his brigadiers – Julian Thompson, Tony Wilson and John Waters (Moore's deputy), Moore pronounced the plan unworkable. The attacks were impossible without artillery support and the guns had to be moved by helicopter from behind Mt Kent to the large, exposed area of ground in the front of this feature before the second phase of the attack could proceed. In order to transport the guns and all the other supplies and equipment required for that phase, the helicopters would be obliged to follow the route past the north end of Mt Kent – a position covered by Mt Longdon, which the Argentines controlled. This left Moore with no option but to move on a broad front.

Having established the objectives in mind, Moore worked out a plan for attacks to be conducted over two successive nights beginning on 11–12 June. 3 Commando Brigade would move first – against Mt Longdon, Two Sisters and Mt Harriet on the first night, followed on the second by both brigades engaged against Tumbledown, Mt William and Wireless Ridge. Success might

induce the Argentines to surrender, but if not, Moore planned to push ahead against Sapper Hill on the third night, thus denying the garrison in Stanley all positions of prominence to the west of the town. By attacking at night, Moore could take advantage of his troops' superior fighting capability and avoid exposure over totally exposed ground to the fire of entrenched defenders armed with rifles, machine guns, mortars and grenades.

It will be recalled that the Task Force had been rushed to the South Atlantic in order, first, to avoid the problems arising out of the UN calling for a ceasefire and subsequent talks; and second, to engage the Argentines before the full onset of winter put a halt to operations and enabled the garrison to remain as a fait accompli. Now, with temperatures steadily dropping, practically all Moore's forces committed to the fight and his supply lines vulnerable, everything depended on a very narrow timetable – a fortnight at the outside – in which to defeat the Argentines and re-establish control over the islands.

LEFT
Loading a 105mm gun of 4 Field Regiment RA under camouflage netting on Sapper Hill, just south-west of Stanley. (Imperial War Museum, FKD 329)

RIGHT
An Argentine soldier armed with a 7.62mm General Purpose Machine Gun occupies a bunker. In what the defenders called the 'Outer Defence Zone' outside Stanley, the rocky ground rendered digging trenches all but impossible. Instead, men resorted to sangars and bunkers. (Imperial War Museum, FKD 2197)

MOUNT LONGDON, 11–12 JUNE

On 11 June, 2 Para flew forward by helicopter from Fitzroy to the west of Mt Kent to take up a lying-up position. Shortly after dusk they moved to higher positions in order to observe the fighting of other units and to be in a position either to support 3 Para on Mt Longdon or 45 Commando on Two Sisters. They now resumed their place in 3 Commando Brigade after being transferred from 5 Infantry Brigade in the wake of the Bluff Cove disaster and the requirement for Wilson to reorganize his forces.

For the attacks on Longdon and Two Sisters, Thompson decided on a night assault – a sensible decision based on a number of considerations. He knew the Argentines controlled all the prominent positions covering the western approaches to Stanley, and appreciated that each could provide mutual support to the others, often with flanking fire. The ground over which his forces had to move was invariably open, highly exposed and easy to defend. It was impossible to be certain of the level of resistance to be encountered, but regular units of the Argentine Army were known to be in the area and even if some of the conscripts could not withstand a determined attack, Thompson had to be careful not to assume victory would come as quickly as it had at Goose Green. He therefore regarded it as vital to capture the three principal mountains – Longdon, Harriet and Two Sisters – in a single coordinated brigade attack. He possessed the necessary units to do so: four highly trained, elite units – 2 and 3 Para, 42 and 45 Commando – all experienced in night-fighting and exceptionally well-motivated.

Ten hours were available for his troops to reach their objectives, and full use of the time available was necessary given the inherent difficulties of moving and fighting over broken ground, which always slowed the advance

Assault by 3 Para on Mt Longdon, 11–12 June

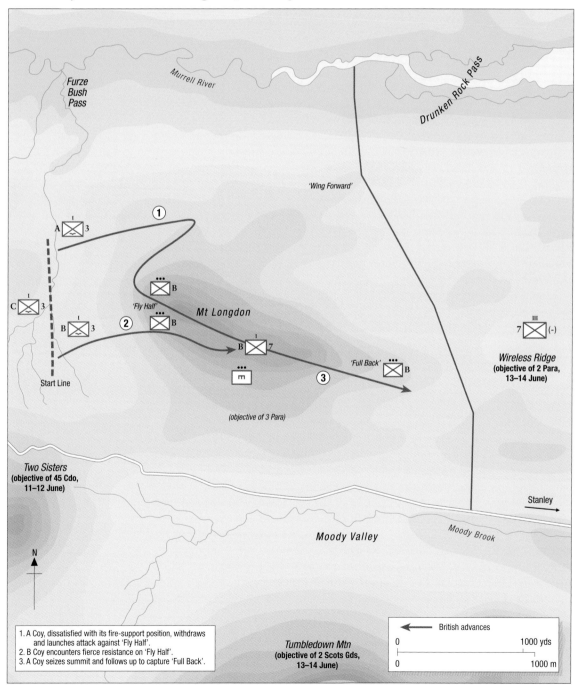

1. A Coy, dissatisfied with its fire-support position, withdraws and launches attack against 'Fly Half'.
2. B Coy encounters fierce resistance on 'Fly Half'.
3. A Coy seizes summit and follows up to capture 'Full Back'.

Men from 3 Para inspecting a captured Argentine command post after the fight for Mt Longdon. The position fell in the wake of fierce fighting and the deployment of anti-tank missiles fired by the battalion's Milans. Mt Tumbledown can be seen in the background. (Imperial War Museum, FKD 2774)

and usually increased the casualty rate. He therefore determined that the attacks should be conducted in silence and without supporting artillery fire, thus preserving, if possible, the element of surprise. Any opponents unfamiliar with fighting at night would be bewildered and less effective and this would be to the attackers' advantage. From approximately 2015hrs, the moonlit night would provide at least a silhouette of the elevated ground, so offering a modicum of direction as 3 Para advanced. Moreover, the attack would be aided by guns of the Royal Artillery, who had 11,000 shells at their disposal, as well as naval gunfire support, consisting of up to 1,400 rounds to be directed by forward observers. Harriers could supply close air support as soon as dawn emerged. As Thompson explained:

> I planned that, by allowing three-quarters of the night for fighting through, the objectives would be secure by dawn. In this way, our assaulting troops would not be exposed to the fire of the Argentine heavy machine guns in the coverless terrain in daylight. Furthermore, it avoided the traditional dawn assault, which I thought the Argentines might expect. I expected that the superior training and quality of our troops would enable them to overcome the opposition in their well-prepared, mountaintop positions. I was not disappointed.

Responsibility for securing Mt Harriet, on 3 Commando Brigade's northern flank, fell to 3 Para, commanded by Lieutenant-Colonel Hew Pike. Having tabbed across East Falkland from San Carlos, the battalion had reached Mount Estancia and the southern slopes of Mt Vernet on 2 June. From there it possessed a dominating view of Stanley from observation posts, while patrols sent out regularly collected intelligence about Argentine strength and dispositions. Men on reconnaissance occasionally clashed with the Argentines, soldiers of B Company, 7th Regiment, though no major encounters took place in the run-up to the main assault. With a week to collect information, those planning the assault on Mt Longdon acquired a fairly clear understanding of the ground to be covered and of the forces opposing them.

Longdon consisted of a long ridge running east to west, with open ground leading up to it from all directions for over 1,000 yards (900m). Minefields, discovered by patrols, lay on the southern flank and reports indicated that the Argentines were well dug in on Wireless Ridge, about 1,000 yards (900m) to the east. Pike had effectively no option but to attack west to east, so avoiding accidental contact with 45 Commando to his right and probably enabling him to isolate the defenders on the western end of the ridge from any potential support from the eastern end. 3 Para proceeded just after nightfall, around 1600hrs. This gave them four hours of movement before the moon rose, providing them with some cover of darkness during their approach to their line of departure, which consisted of a small stream running north–south and therefore perpendicular to their line of attack.

Pike devised a simple plan of attack: two companies forward to be pitted against what he anticipated to be elements of 601 Marine Coy, a well-trained and disciplined unit, and one company of 7th Regiment – in all about 220 men, supported by three 105mm guns at Moody Brook and at least one 155mm on Sapper Hill. Some of the Argentines were equipped with night sights with sufficient intensity to provide a near-daylight view. This, combined with the open ground extending over half a mile from the base of Longdon, offered the defenders an exceptionally good position and offered no option to 3 Para but to cross this expanse before ascending slopes which rose several hundred feet. According to Pike's plan, B Coy would lead the attack by moving straight along the ridge bearing the nickname 'Fly Half' with their objective the eastern spur known as 'Full Back'. At the same time, A Coy, to the left, would advance up the northern spur known as 'Wing Forward'. Once these objectives fell, C Coy, still positioned on the start line with the battalion's 81mm mortars, would proceed to capture Wireless Ridge which lay 1,000 yards (900m) further east, since Thompson desired 'that assaulting units should press on if the opportunity occurred', thus adhering to the doctrine of maintaining the momentum of attack.

The attack got under way 15 minutes late at 2015hrs because of problems in crossing the Murrell River and the absence of 5 and 6 Platoon who got temporarily lost in the total darkness. But the approach proceeded well, with the Paras moving quietly up the slope. The light of the moon soon illuminated the summit and the heights before them, with silence reigning for the moment. Company Sergeant-Major John Weeks, B Coy, described the events that followed:

> It was a very eerie, very quiet, cold night. We were going quite well towards the hill and were 500 metres short of the rock formation, when Corporal Milne trod on a mine. That was the end of our silent night attack. It then became like Guy Fawkes night; I've never seen so many illuminations. I think most of the Argies must have been asleep. But what came at us was bad enough, so if they'd all been awake, they'd have wiped our two platoons off the face of the mountain.

The Argentines responded quickly with artillery fire, but B Coy occupied the western end of Longdon owing to minimal resistance in that sector. Many Argentines were caught completely by surprise, as Cabo Oscar Carrizo of 7th Regiment, recalled:

> I stood and looked down towards the western slope. Then I heard a clunk-click, then many clunk-clicks. I knew that sound. It was bayonets being fixed. Panic surged through my body. I ran to the other bunkers to rouse the men. Many were sound asleep…

Men were scrambling out of their bunkers, Within seconds the whole place was alive with tracer bullets. They whizzed past my head and whacked into the rocks and the ground. Everyone was in a panic. I ran for cover and crawled into a bunker with a sargento. It was impossible to fire my mortar now.

Outside, the English were running past, screaming to each other and firing into tents and bunkers. I could hear my men being killed. They had only just woken up and now they were dying.

If B Coy found the assault against the western end of Longdon much less arduous an affair than expected, they received a much hotter reception on the lower eastern end, where a 105mm gun and heavy machine guns forced the foremost attackers to ground. 4 Platoon cleared an Argentine position and took its gun, but elements of 4 and 5 Platoons became pinned down when they attempted to capture another machine gun and were forced to withdraw. Supporting fire directed in by a forward observer rained down on the defenders, but B Coy's commander, Major M. H. Argue halted the attack to consolidate his position.

Meanwhile, A Coy had proceeded to the left and made its way to the crest of the northern spur, there to find itself under heavy fire from the same defenders blocking B Coy's advance. The Argentines had positioned themselves well, holding points on the reverse slope and supported by well-directed artillery fire. A Coy then passed through B Coy's positions on Fly Half and proceeded towards Full Back with supporting mortar, artillery and machine-gun fire. 1 and 2 Platoons spearheaded the attack, clearing the ridge by ejecting the defenders from their trenches and sangars with small-arms fire, bayonets and grenades, taking prisoners as they advanced towards the eastern end. Ian Moore, A Coy, described the fighting thus:

We took all of our webbing off; we needed to crawl, and British equipment is too bulky to crawl among rocks with. We only kept ammunition, grenades and as much ammunition for the machine-guns as possible. B Company gave us all their belt ammunition and dressings. Only the platoon signaller had any bulky equipment. The tracer from the two Argentinian machine-gun arcs did not meet in the gap but 20 metres back, so we could just get through. Eventually, the whole platoon was through and started moving forward on a 30-metre frontage. Communications were by shouting.

The system worked well. A man called out, then lit up a cigarette behind a rock to signify his location and called for fire on a bearing from him. Then he gave a correction, left or right, up or down, almost like mortar-fire corrections. As soon as an enemy position was spotted, all available fire was brought down in this way. The machine guns did a very good job, often tearing the walls of the sangars apart with 200 or 300 rounds of fire. The Argentinians had made the mistake of filling in the walls with too much turf. When a section was ready to go on with grenades, we called back to the fire-support group to stop; then the men went in in pairs, one covering the other. After about an hour of this, we had removed most of the first group of positions – about a 100 metres in depth, about eight positions destroyed in all.

3 Platoon then advanced through the other two platoons to establish itself on the slope, which extended in the direction of Wireless Ridge slightly to the south-east.

Dawn broke just after the conclusion of the fighting, which had raged for eight hours. Wireless Ridge was beyond the means of 3 Para, for daylight rendered further movement too hazardous, particularly with Tumbledown, immediately to the south, still in the hands of troops capable of offering enfilading fire. Instead, exhausted by their efforts, the Paras dug in on the reverse slopes north-west of Longdon in expectation of a response from Argentine artillery. The rocky outcrops made digging in an arduous affair, so in many cases the troops resorted to constructing sangars to protect themselves from the elements, artillery bombardment and possible counterattack. Meanwhile, efforts were made to clear up the battlefield, which Colour-Sergeant Brian Faulkner described thus:

> It was a typical battlefield mess – entrances to sangars blown away – bodies strewn everywhere; you could see many of their bodies shot as they ran away. What I remember most vividly is the way our bodies were marked by an upturned rifle, stuck into the ground by the bayonet, with a helmet or other identifying mark hung on it. We couldn't reach all of our bodies for several hours because of the shellfire. We didn't bother with theirs; they were just like dummies to us.
>
> Some of the Argie wounded had been injured by phosphorus grenades – severe, deep, burn wounds, very painful. They screamed, were very upset. One or two had bayonet wounds – very unusual in a modern battle – and some were even physically mauled, literally from hand-to-hand fighting with rifle butts or anything that had come to hand.
>
> The Argies had fought very well.

Mount Longdon represented a sound victory for 3 Para, with the Argentines putting up a respectable defence and inflicting a heavy toll of 18 killed and 40 wounded during 3 Para's assault and the shelling that followed. The defenders lost over 50 killed and about the same number as prisoners.

MOUNT HARRIET, 11–12 JUNE

On 31 May 42 Commando had moved by helicopter to Mt Kent, providing them almost two weeks in which to patrol the area around Mt Challenger, Wall Mountain, Goat Ridge and Mt Harriet. By 3 June they were almost certain to be assigned the objective of taking Mt Harriet, a position held by

Attack by 42 Commando on Mt Harriet, 11–12 June

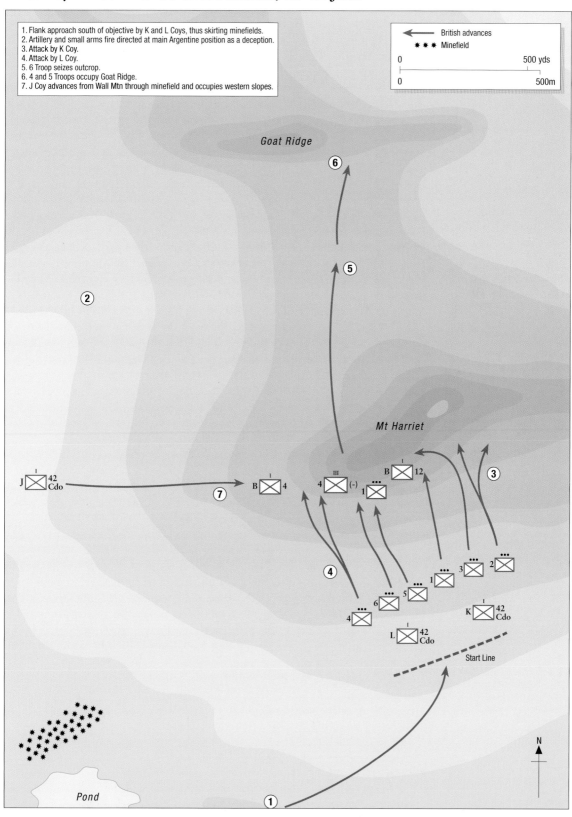

1. Flank approach south of objective by K and L Coys, thus skirting minefields.
2. Artillery and small arms fire directed at main Argentine position as a deception.
3. Attack by K Coy.
4. Attack by L Coy.
5. 6 Troop seizes outcrop.
6. 4 and 5 Troops occupy Goat Ridge.
7. J Coy advances from Wall Mtn through minefield and occupies western slopes.

British advances

✱ ✱ ✱ Minefield

0   500 yds

0   500m

Goat Ridge

Mt Harriet

Pond

Start Line

N

elements of the 4th and 12th Regiments, plus heavy mortars, under Lt. Col. Diego Sona. The patrols provided first-rate intelligence, including the whereabouts of some of the minefields laid by the defenders. However, the commander, Lt. Col. Nick Vaux, had no aerial reconnaissance photographs to assist him and, without these, he had to rely on data about the ground and the strength and disposition of the defenders from material brought back by his patrols, while the gunners attached to 42 Commando made accurate calculations of the height of the feature and the distances for the unit to cover.

Mount Harriet dominated the ground over the track connecting Goose Green and Stanley, which the Argentines had used heavily for resupply. The area was also heavily mined, particularly on the western and southern slopes – the directions from which the Argentines expected to resist an attack. Just north of Harriet lay Goat Ridge, which, although falling within the operational responsibility of 42 Commando, represented its leftmost boundary with 45 Commando, tasked with assaulting Two Sisters. Attempting to take Mt Harriet from the north was deemed too hazardous, with a high probability of 42 Commando coming under fire from its sister unit in the dark. Nor could Vaux responsibly launch a frontal assault over 2,000 yards (1,800m) of open ground, especially when strewn with mines, even under cover of darkness. His plan therefore required more imagination, and represented the most audacious of the three attacks executed that night, with a long march south of the position along its right flank in order to take the position from the rear, capitalizing on intelligence collected by a patrol which had discovered a route unencumbered by mines. Since the Argentines were very likely to have established particularly strong positions at both ends of the mountain, 42 Commando was to assault from the south-east with K Coy spearheading the attack. To do so, they would advance to the south over an extended distance, avoiding the minefields, crossing two tracks and skirting a lake. This route was to be carefully recced and marked and a start line established south-east of Harriet.

The schedule involved 42 Commando crossing the start line at 2030hrs – but over 3 miles (5km) forward of Mt Challenger, at their assembly area. Success depended on approaching in silence and the attack was delayed by an hour owing to the failure of the Recce Platoon of the Welsh Guards, which was to secure the start line, and the leading platoon of 42 Commando, to rendezvous, causing a delay sufficiently long enough for the moon to rise and make the attackers' movements more prominent.

Earlier, J Coy had established its mortars on Mt Wall, while K Coy departed the assembly area at 1730hrs, followed by L Coy an hour later. Unlike the attacks carried out the same night against Mt Longdon and Two Sisters, Vaux planned to dispense with the element of surprise by employing a noisy pre-assault deception plan involving machine-gun and artillery fire directed from the west, organized by J Coy, leaving the impression that this was to be the direction of the main assault.

K Coy, led by Capt. Peter Babbington, crossed the start line at 2200hrs and proceeded 700 yards (640m) up the slopes, after which they encountered Argentine infantry 100 yards (90m) away. Babbington recalled events thus:

> There was a lot of .50 heavy machine-gun fire and assorted small-arms flying around and the rocks were pinging a bit, but you don't actually notice this sort of thing when you're busy trying to control a battle... my Marines started working their way along the ridge; they were making steady progress, about 20 or 30 yards at a time, clearing a position and moving on.

But then artillery came thundering down:

> So we all ran down to the left-hand side into some rocks, and that was a disastrous mistake because we ran right into very concentrated Argentinian artillery fire. That really was quite frightening, horrifically frightening because it's totally impersonal, you've got no control over it, you feel particularly helpless – it's mindless. It's just coming in, 105mm shells landing 4 or 5 feet away from you, the whole ground lifting and bits of splintered rock going winging around. You're just lying curled up by the side of a rock and hoping you're not going to get hit.
>
> I must admit to getting rather edgy about all this shrapnel flying about. We then sort of steadied down for a while because we were now at the end of our part of the objective and the other company was coming up to attack the other end.

Mount Harriet today. A rusted Argentine mortar and shell casings remain behind as some of the few remnants of the struggle between 42 Commando and the Argentine 4th Infantry Regiment. (Imagery provided by RAF Photographic Section, MPC/© UK MoD Crown Copyright 2011)

Despite this heavy fire Vaux's plan succeeded: the Argentines did not anticipate an attack from the rear, though they offered a vigorous resistance nonetheless. As before, the 66mm light anti-tank weapon proved its versatility in destroying Argentine positions among the rocks. Through heavy fighting, K Coy captured the eastern end of Harriet while L Coy took on the forces holding the western end – without the advantage of surprise. Their advance covered more than 600 yards (550m) and required support from Milans to destroy the machine-gun positions. The momentum of attack never faltered: L Coy overran the position and took large numbers of prisoners, including Premier Teniente Ignacio Gorriti of 12th Regiment, who like many of his comrades suffered from faulty weapons and equipment:

> My FAL rifle wasn't working properly; it kept firing three shots at a time; I couldn't make it do single shots and that was the best of three rifles I tried that night! I was making a little counterattack on the flank of the British who

Two Sisters illuminated by a ray of brilliant sunlight penetrating a cloud-covered, darkened sky. (Imagery provided by RAF Photographic Section, MPC/© UK MoD Crown Copyright 2011)

were attacking my men. My radio wasn't working; the wires were all cut by shelling. Our other radios had no batteries. So I could not pass orders to my men – it was just individual action…. A few others and myself took shelter in a hole. Suddenly, I saw three Englishmen against the sky. I didn't open fire; I didn't think it was a time for killing. I asked the men with me whether we should fight on or surrender. They told me to decide. That was very difficult – we surrendered. The British were on top of us; it made no sense at all to keep on fighting.

After eight hours of fighting and the main objective achieved, 42 Commando prepared for an Argentine counterattack, with the next phase to take Goat Ridge which lay half a mile to the north. K Coy led the way as some Argentines abandoned the feature in the darkness while others surrendered by the time the position was in British hands by dawn. No counterattack materialized, but the Marines began to dig in as they came under artillery fire. The fighting had lasted longer than anticipated, leaving no time with which to proceed to their next objective: Mt William. 42 Commando's losses amounted to two killed and 17 wounded. The Argentines lost about ten killed, 53 wounded and a remarkable 250 taken prisoner. Vaux's strategy had succeeded brilliantly, made possible only by troops possessing a high state of fitness, as well as exemplary training in manoeuvring and fighting at night over rugged terrain. 42 Commando had executed a bold attack involving taking the Argentine position from the rear, thereby keeping the casualty rate – one dead and about ten wounded – much lower than that suffered as a result of the frontal attack chosen at Longdon. Vaux later described the men of K Coy, whom he addressed in a protected hollow amongst the crags just after the action ceased:

> They were a moving sight. Weather-beaten, grimy and dishevelled, the Marines formed a ferocious semi-circle around us inhaling wearily on captured cigarettes. I really cannot remember what I said. No doubt it echoed so many similar occasions, when exalted commanders have commended exhausted troops for achievements beyond all expectation. I do remember that I envied them their now-exclusive brotherhood. That belongs only, but always, to those who fight at close quarters alongside one another. Each rifle company would retain that special bond forever. But, if you hadn't been there with them, you could never be a part of it.

Thompson proved correct in pushing the offensive, for winter had well and truly arrived.

Attack by 45 Commando on Two Sisters, 11–12 June

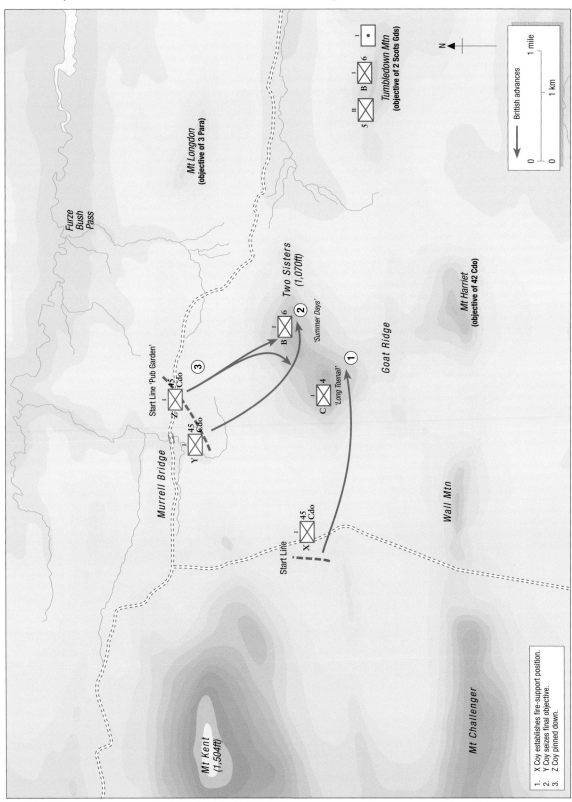

1. X Coy establishes fire-support position.
2. Y Coy seizes final objective.
3. Z Coy pinned down.

TWO SISTERS, 11–12 JUNE

In the centre of the eminences immediately west of Stanley stood Two Sisters, the responsibility for whose capture fell to 45 Commando. The feature consisted of two peaks each of about 1,000ft (300m) in elevation, extending over a mile in length from west to east and notable for its five jagged ridges which formed a ragged spine. Climbing it required particular determination, for the wet rocks and scree slowed progress considerably. One company of conscripts from the 4th and another from the 6th Regiment, which had established a strong defensive position including heavy machine guns and 120mm mortars, held this formidable position.

The commander of 45 Commando, Colonel Andrew Whitehead, laid plans involving an attack in two phases. X Coy, leaving the start line at 2100hrs, was to seize within two hours the ridge known as 'Long Toenail', which lay just south-west of the principal rocky formation, before offering covering fire for the main attack coming from the north-west around Murrell Bridge. This plan would also enable the unit to offer covering fire over Goat Ridge, which acted as the boundary between 45 and 42 Commandos, and prevent the Argentines from occupying that low-lying feature. With 'Long Toenail' secured by X Coy, Z Coy was then to capture the western peak of Two Sisters, followed by Y Coy passing through to seize the eastern eminence known as 'Summer Days'. While the Marines would approach in silence, support was available if necessary from the guns of *Glamorgan* and *Yarmouth*, artillery and the 81mm mortars attached to 45 Commando itself.

On 11 June Whitehead's unit, minus X Coy, left their position behind Mount Kent and, proceeding on a northerly route, arrived at the main start line known as 'Pub Garden' according to schedule. At the same time, X Coy, moving between Mounts Kent and Challenger, arrived at the start line more than two hours late owing to problems encountered during the approach march; specifically, the excessive weight of their equipment – including Milan anti-tank launchers and their 30lb (14kg) ammunition, which represented an immense burden when carried over broken ground. Instead of the expected three hours to reach their start line, Captain Ian Gardiner's company took six – so confirming Clausewitz's dictum that 'friction' sometimes inconveniently imposes itself on operations, unravelling even the most carefully laid plans. Still, the situation proved salvageable, as Gardiner explained, while highlighting an instance of leadership at its best:

> We were 150 very fed-up and tired men – and that was before the real work began. It is miraculous where the reserves of energy can come from. I explained briefly to the Colonel on the radio what the position was. To his everlasting credit, he put me under no unreasonable pressure and said simply, 'Carry on as planned; I will do nothing until I hear from you'. As a result of his patience and understanding, I was able to turn round to my troop commanders and say, 'Put the last six hours right behind you, make your final preparations in your own time, and when you are completely ready, let me know and we will go'. Ten minutes later, 150 men were as good as new and the assault began.

At 2300hrs X Coy began its move over open country towards 'Long Toenail', but halfway up Gardiner and his men were met with bursts of heavy machine-gun fire and were obliged temporarily to withdraw. With Milans and mortar fire directed against these positions, supported by artillery, 2 Troop managed to reach the summit, only to be thrown back by artillery fire before again pushing on, finally to overwhelm the machine-gun positions and secure the feature.

Shortly after midnight, while X Coy was engaged in its struggle for 'Long Toenail', Z Coy, with Y Coy on its right, advanced silently uphill from the start line while the Argentines remained concentrated against X Coy's attack. Once the defenders sent up a flare to illuminate the sky, 8 Troop of Z Coy opened fire, causing such a furious response from the Argentines – including heavy artillery and mortar fire – that the company lost four men killed and the lieutenant ordered a charge against the summit to bring an end to resistance, while at the same time 7 Troop engaged in a heavy exchange of fire while held up by stiff resistance.

On Z Coy's right flank, meanwhile, Y Coy swung in to develop a parallel attack, in so doing silencing some of the machine guns blocking Z Coy's advance. This enabled 8 Troop to proceed further towards the summit with covering fire from 7 Troop, and in due course the two companies cleared the Argentine positions on both the northern and southern sides of the feature. The western section of 'Summer Days' thus fell to Z Coy 2½ hours after it left the start line, while Y Coy passed between the peaks of Two Sisters and proceeded towards the north-eastern summit amidst a shower of small-arms fire. After deploying anti-tank weapons and further hard fighting with its SLRs, 45 Commando prevailed and secured possession of Two Sisters by dawn. As they began to dig in and reorganize, shellfire fell upon their position as Whitehead prepared to move against Mt Tumbledown. Brigadier Thompson considered this unwise and ordered the unit to remain in place, for 5th Infantry Brigade was already poised to take part in the advance on Stanley, with the task of seizing that objective allocated to the Scots Guards.

The fall of Two Sisters represented a serious blow to the Argentine main defences, yet 45 Commando lost only three killed along with one sapper from the Royal Engineers – all from artillery or mortar fire – during the phase when Y and Z Coys were pinned down, plus ten wounded. The Marines took 54 prisoners, of whom 50 were wounded, and killed about ten of the defenders. The remaining Argentines fled eastwards, probably into Stanley. The attackers had received excellent support from the Royal Artillery, who fired about 1,500 rounds.

The three battles of the night of 11–12 June may be seen collectively as a remarkable success for the British, who had defeated a numerically superior force in its main defensive positions. However, the fighting had been more prolonged than expected, rendering impossible further exploitation eastwards. All told, the British suffered 28 fatal casualties and approximately 70 wounded, with a disproportionate share falling on 3 Para, with 19 dead from the difficult frontal assault against Mt Longdon, juxtaposed with the Royal Marines' two assaults which employed flanking approaches which resulted in only five men dead.

Moore had intended to renew his offensive on the following night – 12–13 June – with assaults on Tumbledown Mountain, Mt William and Wireless Ridge, but so rapid a renewal of the fighting could not be undertaken because the Scots Guards and the Gurkhas, tasked to assault Tumbledown and Mt William, respectively, had not completed their reconnaissance and observation. Moore agreed to postpone operations, but only for 24 hours, with the newly available time spent bringing up batteries of artillery and ammunition for both the guns and the infantry. The artillery duly bombarded

45 COMMANDO ATOP TWO SISTERS ENGAGING AN ARGENTINE BUNKER AT CLOSE QUARTERS (pp. 72–73)

Overcoming dug-in defences demanded skilful coordination between attackers variously armed with Self-Loading Rifle **(1)**, L4A2 Light Machine Gun **(2)** and grenade **(3)**, especially in the absence of light anti-tank weapons, which both the Royal Marines and the Paras found extremely effective in the unorthodox role of destroying bunkers such as shown here **(4)**, as well as against trenches, dug-outs and sangars – the last of which consist of embrasures fashioned from rocks where hard ground renders 'digging in' impossible. Note that the Marines have left behind their Bergens, enabling them to fight in much less cumbersome 'Fighting Order': the '58-pattern belt kit (known as 'webbing') and the 'Berghaus Crusader' pack.

But seizing Argentine positions owed as much to the offensive spirit embodied in the ethos of the Royal Marines as to their weapons and equipment, as confirmed in an account by Sergeant George Matthews:

The point section was just cresting a ridge line, when they [the Argentines] opened up and the guys immediately went to ground. The first volley of heavy machine-gun fire went over their heads…

Even though they opened up too early, the weight of fire was so heavy that we were stuck; we couldn't get over this little hummock. It was coming from heavy machine guns on the top. One was engaging Yankee and Zulu Companies and the other one was engaging us and we were channelled. Everywhere we tried to go, the rock channelled you towards these machine guns…

Young Dave O'Connor… suddenly leapt forward with his machine gun, screaming, 'You Argie bastards!' He went over the rocks, totally exposed, yet followed by his number two who carried the ammunition. They dived down on the rock and commenced to open fire at this machine gun. For a couple of seconds it was just our machine gun… and theirs… and then he went into the open under heavy fire, continually engaging this machine gun. That drew their fire for a second and in that second another young lad, barely out of training, jumped up with a 66mm rocket launcher, fired it at their machine-gun position and hit just above. He stayed there in the open, shouting for another which was thrown to him, fired, and it smashed in close to the machine gun. For a split second the fire stopped and we just lifted, off we went…

After we'd taken the machine gun out, there were a couple left further up, on the way to the other peak. The guys took them out with grenades and rifles, and the way they did it was amazing. We practise clearing enemy positions just as we practise house clearing: it's a very similar drill, in fact. The grenade goes in first and then, after the explosion, in you go, firing a few rounds into the building. The point section did exactly the same to clear all the little rock positions. The lads up there were working in pairs. One would throw in a grenade, the other would charge in, fire a few rounds, shout 'Clear!' and then move on to the next one. It was so ingrained, and shows that the training does work – it was second nature.

Argentine positions, with returning fire killing four soldiers on Mt Longdon. At the same time, the Argentines conducted air raids on 13 June to assist their harried forces on the ground, striking 3 Commando Brigade's HQ near Mt Kent with Skyhawks, as well as 2 Para's positions near Mt Longdon. There were no British losses, apart from damage to three helicopters and delays caused to 2 Para's efforts to prepare for the following evening's attack. The RAF answered in turn, with Harrier strikes against Argentine artillery positions using laser-guided 1,000lb bombs, with devastating effect.

On the evening of 13 June the offensive resumed, with the main effort to come from 5 Infantry Brigade in the south against the Stanley defences, involving 2 Scots Guards against Tumbledown Mountain and 1/7 Gurkhas against Mt William. Further north, 2 Para, which had been transferred back to 3 Commando Brigade, was tasked with assaulting Wireless Ridge. The Royal Artillery would furnish five batteries of guns to support these three attacks, together with four warships and eight light tanks of the Blues and Royals which had proceeded across the island from San Carlos.

MOUNT TUMBLEDOWN, 13–14 JUNE

Tumbledown constituted a very formidable position held by a garrison consisting of elements of the 5th Marines – perhaps the best sizeable unit the Argentines possessed on the islands – holding the key post in the defences west of Stanley. Two companies stood on the mountain itself, with troops also deployed on Mt William and to the south near the track leading into the capital.

As a prelude, the Mountain and Arctic Warfare Cadre of the Royal Marines had already scouted the area and acquired valuable intelligence on the area west of Tumbledown. Opening moves began on the morning of 13 June, when helicopters conveyed the Scots Guards from Bluff Cove to the western end of Goat Ridge, there to be briefed extensively on Argentine strength and dispositions. In his assessment, the battalion's commander, Lt. Col. Scott, thought that an attack across the exposed southern slopes of the mountain posed too great a risk to his unit, so he instead chose a western advance along the summit ridge without the benefit of supporting fire, thereby ensuring as quiet an approach as possible. In phase one, a diversionary raid carried out along the Fitzroy–Stanley track would precede G Coy's seizure of the western end of the eminence, while in the second phase, Left Flank (LF) Coy was to proceed through G Coy and capture the area around the summit. Lastly, Right Flank (RF) Coy would skirt round LF Coy to take the eastern end.

LEFT
Argentine troops from the 5th Marines on Mt Tumbledown. On 13–14 June, together with survivors from B Coy, 6th Regiment, which had fled Two Sisters, they offered serious resistance to the assault of 2 Scots Guards, not only driving off the diversionary attack from the west but holding up the main thrust for four hours, pinning the Guardsmen down with accurate artillery fire until finally overwhelmed by a series of coordinated attacks; even then the Argentines contested the summit. (Imperial War Museum, FKD 2933)

RIGHT
7 Platoon, G Coy, 2 Scots Guards on Mt Tumbledown learn of the Argentine surrender at dawn on 14 June. (Imperial War Museum, FKD 314)

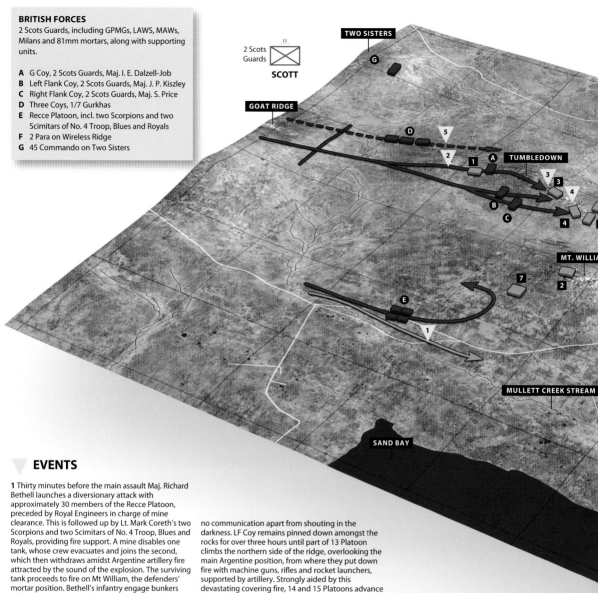

BRITISH FORCES

2 Scots Guards, including GPMGs, LAWS, MAWs, Milans and 81mm mortars, along with supporting units.

A G Coy, 2 Scots Guards, Maj. I. E. Dalzell-Job
B Left Flank Coy, 2 Scots Guards, Maj. J. P. Kiszley
C Right Flank Coy, 2 Scots Guards, Maj. S. Price
D Three Coys, 1/7 Gurkhas
E Recce Platoon, incl. two Scorpions and two Scimitars of No. 4 Troop, Blues and Royals
F 2 Para on Wireless Ridge
G 45 Commando on Two Sisters

2 Scots Guards

SCOTT

TWO SISTERS

GOAT RIDGE

TUMBLEDOWN

MT. WILLIA

MULLETT CREEK STREAM

SAND BAY

▼ EVENTS

1 Thirty minutes before the main assault Maj. Richard Bethell launches a diversionary attack with approximately 30 members of the Recce Platoon, preceded by Royal Engineers in charge of mine clearance. This is followed up by Lt. Mark Coreth's two Scorpions and two Scimitars of No. 4 Troop, Blues and Royals, providing fire support. A mine disables one tank, whose crew evacuates and joins the second, which then withdraws amidst Argentine artillery fire attracted by the sound of the explosion. The surviving tank proceeds to fire on Mt William, the defenders' mortar position. Bethell's infantry engage bunkers with rifles and grenades, losing two dead and seven wounded, but killing ten before wandering into a minefield, from which engineers later extricate them.

2 Amidst a clear and calm, though bitterly cold, night G Coy under Maj. Dalzell-Job silently approaches the western end of the main ridge, discovers two unmanned machine-gun posts and occupies the first objective – the first third of Tumbledown– without opposition.

3 Left Flank Coy under Maj. John Kiszley moves against the middle third of Tumbledown, where all remains quiet for the first 30 minutes until the defenders unleash a thunderous, continuous hail of small arms fire directed with the aid of night sights. Attackers are forced to take cover amidst crags with

no communication apart from shouting in the darkness. LF Coy remains pinned down amongst the rocks for over three hours until part of 13 Platoon climbs the northern side of the ridge, overlooking the main Argentine position, from where they put down fire with machine guns, rifles and rocket launchers, supported by artillery. Strongly aided by this devastating covering fire, 14 and 15 Platoons advance through the Argentine positions.

4 Right Flank Coy under Maj. Price follows up LF Coy's advance, deploying 1 Platoon high up in the rocks to the north in order to offer fire support, while 2 and 3 Platoons begin the main attack with a right hook over fairly open ground. Advancing by half sections, the company clears trenches, sangars and machine-gun positions. With six men wounded but no fatalities, RF Coy captures the final eminence – over 11 hours after the Guardsmen had crossed their Start Line.

5 Three coys of 1/7 Gurkhas under Lt. Col. David Morgan proceed with the intention of attacking Mt William, suffering in the process eight wounded from shell and mortar fire. Owing to approaching dawn the attack is not pressed home.

6 2 Para attacks Wireless Ridge on the same evening.

7 Argentines flee Tumbledown.

8 Argentines abandon Mt William.

9 Marines from 40 Cdo, attached to the Welsh Guards, are helicoptered in for the last fight, with M Coy, 5th Marines, on Sapper Hill, a grassy 140m (450ft) eminence only a mile south-west of Stanley.

ATTACK OF 2 SCOTS GUARDS ON MT TUMBLEDOWN, 13–14 JUNE

Following the capture of Mt Longdon, Mt Harriet and Two Sisters the previous day, Tumbledown constituted the key remaining position in the Argentine defences around Stanley.

Note: Gridlines are shown at intervals of 1km/0.62miles

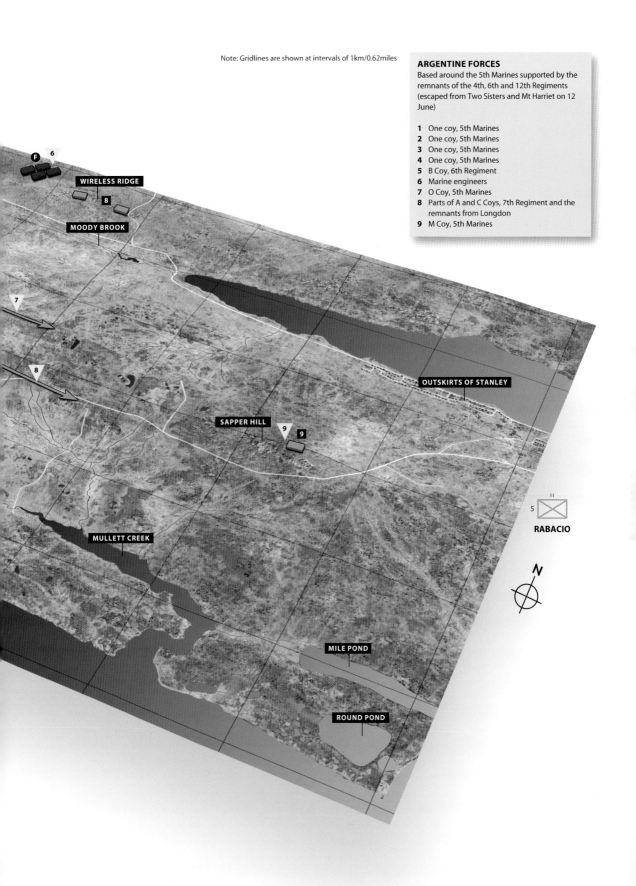

ARGENTINE FORCES
Based around the 5th Marines supported by the remnants of the 4th, 6th and 12th Regiments (escaped from Two Sisters and Mt Harriet on 12 June)

1 One coy, 5th Marines
2 One coy, 5th Marines
3 One coy, 5th Marines
4 One coy, 5th Marines
5 B Coy, 6th Regiment
6 Marine engineers
7 O Coy, 5th Marines
8 Parts of A and C Coys, 7th Regiment and the remnants from Longdon
9 M Coy, 5th Marines

WIRELESS RIDGE

MOODY BROOK

OUTSKIRTS OF STANLEY

SAPPER HILL

RABACIO

MULLETT CREEK

MILE POND

ROUND POND

N

Mount Tumbledown. Characteristic of the other features immediately west of Stanley, note the treeless, utterly exposed ground – a considerable disadvantage to an attacker. (Imagery provided by RAF Photographic Section, MPC/© UK MoD Crown Copyright 2011)

The diversion began at 2030hrs and half an hour later G Coy began their advance amidst freezing conditions. Supported by light tanks, the diversionary group engaged the Argentines for two hours and suffered one Guardsman and one Royal Engineer killed, with others wounded when the men withdrew across a minefield – but their action succeeded in its purpose. By this time, G Coy had crossed the Start Line and took its first objective by 2230hrs, whereupon this new ground served to support LF Coy who encountered serious resistance from snipers and machine guns. Hard fighting followed, involving anti-armour weapons against Argentine bunkers, with progress still severely held up despite the efforts of Guardsmen to use grenades at perilously close range. Around 0230hrs the attackers called in artillery support in order to break the impasse, which required several instances of hand-to-hand combat. A handful of men from LF Coy finally reached the summit – but only after a seven-hour fight, complete with bayonets blooded.

In the third and final phase of the battle, RF Coy advanced, making extensive use of its 84mm Carl Gustav anti-armour weapons and LAWs as Sergeant McGuinness relates:

> I saw three sangars 50 metres away to the left and asked the platoon commander by radio for the '84' team to come up. It was snowing by now. They fired at the first sangar but missed; the snow was blurring his sights. I took it off him; I had done a 'Skill at Arms Course' at Warminister so could judge the distance without a sight. I fired three rounds at those sangars and scored three hits. I think we blew the sangars and possibly the men over the back of the steep side of the ridge. On the third shot, I actually hit an Argentinian who had been putting his head up and down. He just disintegrated.

Fighting did not cease until about 0815hrs on the 14th, long after sunrise, in the course of which the Scots Guards suffered seven killed – two during the diversion and five in the main assault, plus a further two from mortar fire when shells landed while the men tended the wounded. It took just over 11 hours from the moment they left their Start Line for the Guardsmen to wrest the ridge from the Argentines, of whom 34 were made prisoner and *c*.40 killed. It represented a significant achievement, though it took much longer than the plan envisioned since the best Argentine units were deployed there and little remained in the path of the British offensive. With the fall of Tumbledown went the key feature in the Argentine defence of Stanley. Only Mt William and Wireless Ridge stood in the path of the British offensive.

Meanwhile, the Gurkhas awaited their turn to enter the fray, having formed up to begin their attack on Mt William, which could not begin until the Scots Guards completed their occupation of Tumbledown. However, once it became clear that the fight for Tumbledown would proceed through the night, Wilson ordered the Gurkhas to advance, though in the event they suffered bitter disappointment when they discovered the defenders had fled, leaving the abandoned feature littered with detritus and denying the Gurkhas a full share in the fighting.

WIRELESS RIDGE, 13–14 JUNE

Two miles (3km) to the north-east of Tumbledown lay Wireless Ridge, the objective for 2 Para, the only major unit already to have fought in a principal engagement. Wireless Ridge in fact consisted of two separate pieces of high ground, which Lt. Col. David Chaundler, Jones's successor, decided to attack from the north. Whereas 2 Para had had relatively little fire support at Goose Green, quite the reverse prevailed at Wireless Ridge. It was supported by two batteries of artillery through the course of the night, with other guns available from the Royal Artillery if needed, as well as the firepower of HMS *Ambuscade*, plus mortars fired by 3 Para and those attached to 2 Para itself. Finally, two Scorpions and two Scimitars of the Blues and Royals were available, capable of offering close support since the ground offered no steep sides. Opposing 2 Para were A and G Coys, 7th Regiment, plus the remnants of B Coy which had fought 3 Para on Mt Longdon. The defenders had at their disposal snipers, heavy machine guns, mortars and artillery.

LEFT
Soldiers of 1/7 Gurkhas unloading a Chinook. The Gurkhas, part of the regular establishment of the British Army, are tough, hardy, highly trained soldiers from Nepal. They were severely disappointed not to play a more active role in operations, which for them consisted only of clearing a few Argentines from Lafonia and occupying Mt William after the defenders had fled. (Mary Evans Picture Library, 10097144)

RIGHT
Major-General Jeremy Moore, commander of British land forces on the Falklands, bearing the instrument of surrender signed by Brig. Gen. Menéndez. (Imperial War Museum, FKD 430)

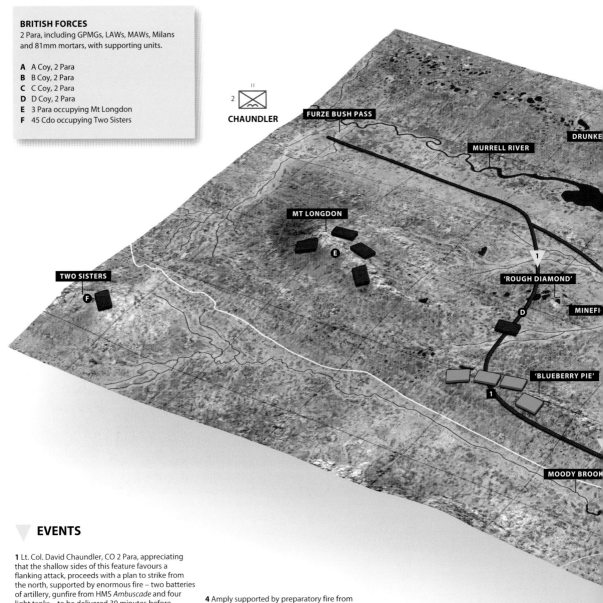

2 CHAUNDLER

FURZE BUSH PASS

DRUNKE

MURRELL RIVER

MT LONGDON

E

TWO SISTERS

F

'ROUGH DIAMOND'

1

D

MINEFI

'BLUEBERRY PIE'

1

MOODY BROOK

▼ EVENTS

1 Lt. Col. David Chaundler, CO 2 Para, appreciating that the shallow sides of this feature favours a flanking attack, proceeds with a plan to strike from the north, supported by enormous fire – two batteries of artillery, gunfire from HMS *Ambuscade* and four light tanks – to be delivered 30 minutes before infantry contact. At 0945hrs, aided by machine guns from the Blues and Royals and artillery fire, D Coy attacks 'Rough Diamond', the first objective, probably held by the Argentine reserve, since the main body is facing south. The defenders retreat, leaving a few dead. D Coy suffers no fatalities.

2 A and B Coys, further to the east of D Coy, advance against the next objective, 'Apple Pie', with machine-gun, artillery and tank fire driving off most of the defenders before the infantry make contact.

3 C Coy follows up the success of A and B Coys, and occupies the abandoned Argentine position.

4 Amply supported by preparatory fire from *Ambuscade* and two batteries of artillery, D Coy launches an attack from west to east, rolling up the long, southern outcrop nicknamed 'Blueberry Pie'. Fire from the four light tanks and Milan anti-tank rockets directed against the defenders' right flank helps expel the Argentines from the first half of the ridge, but the defenders strongly contest possession of the remainder before fleeing in the direction of Moody Brook.

5 3rd, 6th and 25th Regiments in Stanley and at the airfield – together with all other Argentine forces on both East and West Falkland – surrender on the 14th according to agreed terms.

ASSAULT BY 2 PARA ON WIRELESS RIDGE, 13–14 JUNE

The struggle for Wireless Ridge proved nearly as difficult for the British as the capture of Tumbledown about a mile away. 2 Para's objectives consisted of two parallel ridges running east–west, with the southern one reaching a height of 300ft (90m). As such the feature did not pose as formidable a challenge in terms of height or rockiness as Tumbledown.

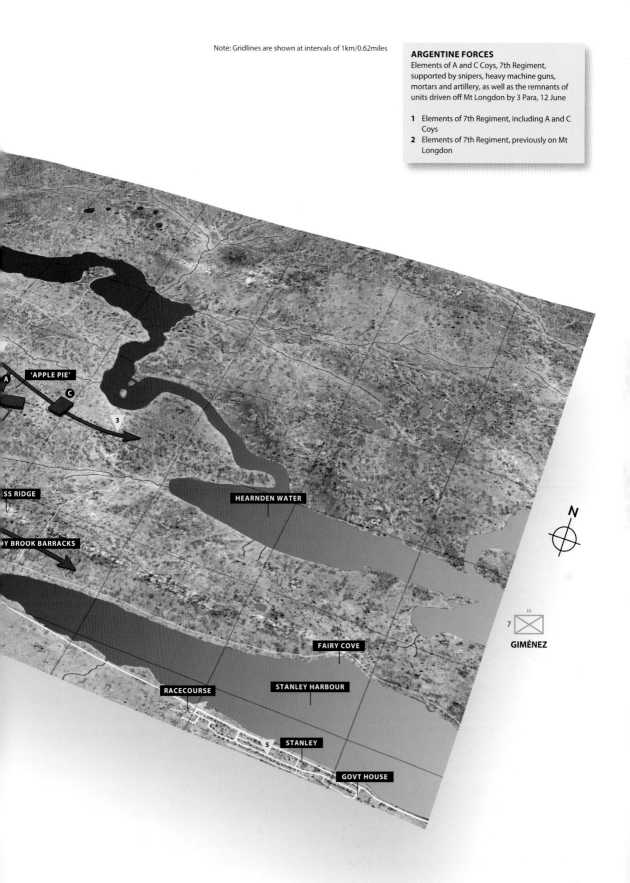

Note: Gridlines are shown at intervals of 1km/0.62miles

A

'APPLE PIE'

C

3

SS RIDGE

HEARNDEN WATER

Y BROOK BARRACKS

N

7 GIMÉNEZ

FAIRY COVE

RACECOURSE

STANLEY HARBOUR

5 STANLEY

GOVT HOUSE

Naval Party 8901, the Royal Marines garrison of the Falkland Islands evicted by the Argentine invaders, prepare to raise the Falkland Islands flag outside Government House after the Argentine surrender. (Imperial War Museum, FKD 2049)

Chaundler divided his plan into four phases to include preparatory artillery fire. In the first phase, D Coy was to assault 'Rough Diamond', an occupied position slightly to the north of the main objective and north-east of Mt Longdon. In the second phase, A and B Coys were to capture 'Apple Pie', also north of the main feature. Once 'Rough Diamond' had fallen, D Coy would move in the course of phase three to seize the whole of Wireless Ridge, nicknamed 'Blueberry Pie', from west to east, supported by fire provided by A and B Coys. In the fourth and final phase, C Coy would march east before taking the westernmost contour, which rose a mere 100ft (30m) above the valley.

Having concluded its march from Furze Bush Pass on the evening of 13 June, 2 Para prepared to assault Wireless Ridge as supporting fire opened on 'Rough Diamond' at 2115hrs. Half an hour later D Coy left the start line, supported by the Scimitars and Scorpions. On reaching 'Rough Diamond' D Coy discovered the defenders, minus a few killed, had withdrawn under the weight of incoming fire, but while the Paras sought to consolidate this newly occupied ground, they themselves became the target of an artillery barrage, in this case 155mm guns. At this point, to the east, A and B Coys began their advance from the start line, suffering in the process one soldier killed by artillery fire. The two companies approached 'Apple Pie' and prepared to engage the defenders, when the Argentines, bowing to the pressure of the combination of artillery, mortar and machine-gun fire directed against their position, withdrew, enabling C Coy rapidly to occupy ring contour 100 without meeting any resistance.

Moving on from 'Rough Diamond', D Coy then proceeded to the western end of Wireless Ridge and prepared to assault across the length of the feature at the same time as the light tanks of the Blues and Royals, situated on 'Apple Pie' with A and B Coys, offered supporting fire, together with the Para's Milans and machine guns. D Coy succeeded in seizing the first half of the ridge with little effort, but the defenders offered stubborn resistance over the remaining half, with the Paras obliged to clear one bunker after the next. Their advance never faltered, however, and eventually the defence collapsed, leaving D Coy in possession of the ridge. The victors then began to dig in and, as in the wake of other operations conducted that day, the Argentines bombarded their lost position with shellfire through the night. At the same time, 2 Para, perceiving the Argentines regrouping in the area of Moody Brook under the cover of darkness, prepared for a possible counterattack.

As anticipated, at daybreak a small force of Argentines assaulted D Coy's position, only to be repulsed by the defenders and their supporting fire from mortars and the 105mm guns of the Royal Artillery. As the sun rose higher the Argentines fled in the direction of Stanley as 2 Para, having lost two men killed by friendly artillery fire and another by Argentine small-arms fire, urged Thompson to allow them to follow up their victory and advance east. The Argentine losses may have numbered as high as 100, plus 17 prisoners. The rest ran off, probably into Stanley.

Unlike at Goose Green, at Wireless Ridge 2 Para had encountered comparatively little resistance, received significant fire support from tanks and artillery and had learned from the hard experience of a fortnight before. Chaundler explained the difference that prevailed once half the position lay in his hands:

> By that stage, everything was going well. Communications were good and I realized how effective the supporting fire was. It is very difficult for peacetime soldiers to appreciate this, but the battalion had Goose Green behind us by now and it [Wireless Ridge] was an essentially all-arms battle and we were able to achieve our objectives with minimum casualties.
>
> It was also a battle of manoeuvre in which we attacked the enemy from different directions and on different axes, so they never did know what was coming at them. That was the difference between doing something for the first and for the second time. Because we had Goose Green behind us, there was a different attitude in the battalion and, while the soldiers were more apprehensive, they were also much more professional because they knew what was going to happen and this was essentially why a quite ambitious plan worked so well.

The fall of Wireless Ridge and Mt Tumbledown broke the back of the Argentine defensive network near Stanley and, on 14 June, in defiance of Galtieri's orders to hold out, Menéndez agreed to a ceasefire, his outright surrender becoming effective at 2059hrs local time. Moore, perhaps with an eye to posterity, sent a signal back to London: 'The Falkland Islands are once more under the government desired by their inhabitants. God Save the Queen'.

Mount Tumbledown, located just 4 miles (6km) from the outskirts of Stanley. (UK MOD/Crown Copyright 2012)

AFTERMATH

British service personnel suffered 252 fatal casualties and 777 wounded across all services engaged – Army, Royal Marines, Royal Navy, Royal Air Force, the Royal Fleet Auxiliary and the Merchant Navy. Three Falkland islanders were also killed. Of this total, the Royal Marines lost 26 killed and the Army 148 personnel. The Task Force as a whole lost four warships and a landing craft, one fleet auxiliary and one merchantman. Helicopter losses amounted to 23 from the Royal Navy, seven from the RAF, three from the Royal Marines and one from the Army.

Argentine fatalities amounted to about 750, of whom 261 served in the army and 37 in the marines. In addition, approximately 1,100 personnel were wounded or fell ill. Well-documented figures for Argentine prisoners reveal that 12,978 personnel fell into British hands during the whole spectrum of operations from the recapture of South Georgia to the surrender of South Thule in the South Sandwich Islands, c.1,000 miles (1,600km) south-east of the Falklands.

A number of key factors can be identified as having contributed to the belligerents' success and failure on the ground. It is instructive first to examine the principal errors committed by the British before considering the virtues of their enterprise. By irresponsibly concentrating so many of their heavy-lift helicopters in the hold of the *Atlantic Conveyor* the British denied themselves that vital element of mobility fundamental to maintaining operations across ground inaccessible to all but tracked and off-road vehicles, of which, notably, the Task Force possessed almost none – rendering heliborne transport almost indispensable. Sufficient numbers of helicopters remained to convey a portion of the forces detailed to the southern flank of Moore's offensive, but only the remarkable degree of fitness possessed by the Paras and Marines enabled him to continue to pursue his basic strategy – the eastward push on Stanley. In truth, most units simply could not have 'yomped' or 'tabbed' the distances achieved, in the time desired and with loads required. Meanwhile, at home, the British earmarked woefully inadequate reserves. However quickly they might have been deployed to the Falklands *in extremis*, the introduction of a single battalion was unlikely either to turn the tide or stabilize a crisis which could amount to nothing more than what in military parlance is known as 'reinforcing failure' – the act of attempting to recover a dire situation by introducing further troops when in fact it is irrecoverable, compounding one's error by foolishly involving the reinforcements in the fate of other troops for whom defeat is inevitable. In intelligence-gathering operations otherwise generally successful, a few failures emerged; notably the radical underestimation of the strength of the Argentine garrison in the Darwin–Goose Green area by the SAS.

On the other hand, the British adopted a clearly conceived strategy and employed well-executed tactics. They appreciated from the outset the necessity of landing unopposed and rapidly establishing a safe, easily defended beachhead, and while they chose one on the opposite side of the island from their ultimate objective, San Carlos still lay sufficiently close to Stanley to serve its purpose as an entrêpot for supplies before 3 Commando Brigade and 5 Infantry Brigade could establish forward bases at Teal Inlet and Bluff Cove respectively. Careful planning went into choosing the most suitable landing sites, based heavily on the superb pre-war coastal surveys conducted by Major Ewen Southby-Tailyour RM. From the outset the British seized the initiative on the ground and maintained a swift tempo of operations, forcing the Argentines to become reactive instead of proactive. The raid on Pebble Island, conducted even before the landings at San Carlos, epitomized the aggressiveness with which British forces prosecuted the campaign as a whole.

At the tactical level, they appreciated that the barren terrain of the Falklands provided so little natural cover that attacking troops operating over large distances made themselves vulnerable to machine-gun and artillery fire. Battalion commanders recognized that attacking under the cover of darkness, whilst slowing movement, would greatly mitigate these disadvantages, enabling soldiers trained in moving and fighting at night to approach their objectives with a degree of protection.

The British Government, in dispatching the Task Force without delay, demonstrated from the outset its determination to reclaim the islands by force if necessary, a determination which set the mood for the troops, whose commanders understood from the outset that success depended on defeating the Argentine garrison and retaking Stanley. Crucially, the principle of 'selection and maintenance of the aim', so ingrained in British Army doctrine, remained paramount throughout. Moreover, the British made the correct decision to strike at Goose Green early in order to pre-empt any Argentine thrust against San Carlos and to secure an early victory, which thereby boosted morale within the forces, strengthened public opinion and bolstered the government's commitment to pursue the campaign vigorously.

A thorough consideration of the factors underpinning success and failure in the South Atlantic must also take into account the Argentine perspective.

Argentine strategy on the ground suffered from a number of fatal flaws: Menéndez hesitated to respond for several days after British forces came ashore at San Carlos, when he might have prolonged the campaign by

LEFT
Royal Marines of 45 Commando, some carrying Bergens and weapons weighing between 100 and 140lbs (45–65kg), arrive in Stanley in the wake of their victory at Two Sisters. (Imperial War Museum, FKD 2040)

RIGHT
Weapons training for Royal Marines aboard a Royal Fleet Auxiliary vessel during the voyage to the South Atlantic. During their many weeks at sea soldiers and marines also maintained their high state of physical fitness by following a strict exercise regime which included running laps around the perimeter of their vessels. (Imperial War Museum, FKD 2200)

launching anything from a major raid, a reconnaissance in force or a proper counterattack employing, for instance, the sizeable forces deployed at Goose Green. Even without a major counterattack against the beachhead, he almost certainly would have held up the course of the campaign, thereby stretching the timeline into the depths of winter and forcing to a standstill an adversary thus robbed of maritime support owing to heavy seas and high winds.

It is also important to appreciate that had the Argentines defended the western approach to Stanley with greater tenacity – or at least held the mountains with greater, better-supplied numbers – Moore's offensive might have been blunted long enough to alter fundamentally the outcome of the campaign. The British had committed virtually all their ground strength to this offensive, with only a modicum of a reserve available: half of 40 Commando based at San Carlos and a company of Gurkhas at Goose Green. Their forces west of Stanley had thus far suffered only minimal losses through exposure and trench foot, but they simply could not remain in place for long while winter conditions grew steadily worse. Maintaining his infantry and artillery in place would have necessitated calling up his reserves from San Carlos and Goose Green, thereby exposing his unprotected rear to attack from the garrison on West Falkland or from fresh forces dispatched by air from the mainland to land at the airfield at Goose Green.

While it is true that Britain still possessed large numbers of troops elsewhere – albeit divided principally between garrisons in the UK, Germany, Cyprus and Brunei – no reinforcements were in transit, and any on standby, such as the 1st Queen's Own Highlanders, though certainly capable of reaching Ascension unharmed, would then have had to land at the airstrip at Goose Green under the risk of air attack. In short, the overall success of the British effort depended on rapid success in the mountains in front of Stanley, for failure might have obliged the Thatcher government to negotiate a compromise settlement to include a complete withdrawal of British forces.

The Argentines need not have regarded British ground forces as the Clausewitzian 'centre of gravity'; merely concentrating its air, sea and land assets on their opponents' extremely vulnerable logistics might have rendered British operations untenable. Alternatively, a decisive strike against a major troopship such as the *QE2* or *Canberra*, or one of the two aircraft carriers alone might have obliged Britain to suspend or cancel operations. By failing either to resist the initial landings at San Carlos Water or to disrupt the later establishment of a logistics centre at Teal Inlet and Fitzroy Bay, the Argentines missed more than one opportunity to delay or possibly even severely disrupt the drive on Stanley, leaving the onset of winter to force a ceasefire and a negotiated settlement. Finally, Menéndez engaged in regular disputes with Brigadier-Generals Joffre and Daher in Stanley, centring around the means of, first, repelling the landing force and, thereafter, defending the capital.

The Argentines laid their minefields without proper consideration of their opponents' line of approach, thus enabling the British to circumvent them easily during the attacks on Mt Harriet and Two Sisters. At the strategic level, the Argentines adopted a flawed strategy that committed the most numerous and best-quality troops to the Stanley sector, thereby failing to anticipate the possible need to oppose a landing elsewhere. Beyond the capital their dispositions appeared quite sound, with concentrations around the airfield at Goose Green and of course in the mountains defending the western approach to Stanley. Nevertheless, some of these defensive positions the Argentines established in an illogical fashion or neglected altogether, such as at the western end of Longdon where they failed to entrench themselves, defying military logic by rendering vulnerable the point upon which any assault would likely fall. Tactical blunders occurred elsewhere: Argentine positions at Goose Green did not extend far enough to prevent 2 Para from outflanking them, notwithstanding the fact that an otherwise eminently defensible narrow isthmus ought to have rendered a frontal assault over open ground, with clear fields of fire and over twice the number of defenders, virtually impregnable.

Finally, Argentine dispositions on West Falkland served very little purpose, apart from monitoring naval activity in Falkland Sound and possibly interdicting flights over its airspace. Nearly 20 per cent of the Argentine garrison on the Falklands occupied the two main positions on West Falkland, which most strategists would immediately reject as a potential springboard for a British attack against East Falkland since landings there must inevitably require a second amphibious operation. In the event, troops on West Falkland, which possessed little of strategic value except the airstrip at Pebble Island – which in any event the SAS had already destroyed a week before the main landings – played no role in operations to the east, rendering the *c.*1,700 troops there effectively impotent.

Men of 40 Commando Royal Marines raise the Union Flag on West Falkland after the Argentine surrender. (Imperial War Museum, FKD 435)

Royal Marines in full kit entering Stanley. (Royal Marines Museum)

While the Argentines very sensibly stockpiled large quantities of food, ammunition and clothing in Stanley, serious flaws in the distribution system, exacerbated by the corrupt practice of raiding or stealing the troops' ration packs and parcels from home, left those troops most in need of such sustenance and *matériel* suffering from serious shortages. Inefficiency and a lack of off-road vehicles left troops in the mountains effectively stranded even while in sight of the capital. In short, at best the Argentine logistic system suffered from poor foresight and, at worst, shocking mismanagement. If UK forces struggled with an exceptionally long supply line – 20 times longer than their adversaries – the Argentines, with only 400 miles (650km) to traverse, still managed lamentably, failing to appreciate that supplies earmarked for one brigade for 30 days could not remotely hope to serve the needs of a garrison facing the possibility of having to defend the islands. When in response to the dispatch of the Task Force the junta sent considerable reinforcements, bolstering the garrison to over 11,000 troops, it failed to provide both the requisite amount of supplies and appropriate clothing for their period of occupation – less than three months – and made inadequate provision for their distribution.

Although unquantifiable, the high state of British morale clearly bore a heavy influence on operations, for while the typical Argentine soldier strongly supported the national cause of 'recovering the Malvinas', there seems little doubt that his British counterpart adhered to his country's own moral position with at least equal fervour. Men almost invariably fight for the sake of their comrades rather than for lofty principles, but a strong belief pervaded the Task Force that the infringement of sovereign rights and the principle of self-determination could not go unchallenged. As Moore himself summed it up: 'The basic difference was that they were fighting for the islands; we were fighting for the islanders'. Throughout the campaign, the British objective remained clear and unambiguous; the means deployed proportionate; and the overwhelming majority of the public stood behind government policy and the armed forces, the latter of whom harboured few doubts about the justice of the cause in the defence of which the nation called them.

Conversely, despite the initial euphoria experienced by Argentine forces in the Falklands prior to the commencement of hostilities at sea – but more particularly prior to the sinking of the *Belgrano* – the garrison's morale suffered from the early realization that government claims about the readiness of the islanders to receive them as liberators were false and, worse still, amounted to more cynical propaganda from a regime already made infamous by its clampdown on internal dissent and the arrest and disappearance of tens of thousands of its citizens. This consideration, coupled with the blows to morale inflicted by the Goose Green disaster and the privations suffered by ill-equipped and hungry troops in the mountains, numbered amongst the numerous factors which contributed to Argentine defeat.

Argentina's failure to deploy her best troops to prevent repossession of the Falklands stands high amongst the catalogue of errors committed by the strategists in Buenos Aires. The best available unit, 5th Marines, fought well on Tumbledown, but the garrison as a whole ought to have included a strong proportion of picked units, including commandos otherwise deployed on the Argentine mainland to deter Chilean intervention at a moment of vulnerability. In the event, most of the Argentine forces, notwithstanding their greater numbers, comprised at best professional soldiers of ordinary quality; at worst, raw recruits of negligible value, even when firmly ensconced in entrenched positions with the expectation of conducting nothing more substantial than a static defence and small-scale local counterattacks. In short, once driven from a position, the Argentines exhibited a remarkable degree of passivity, making no effort to reorganize and contest possession of lost ground, to say nothing of seeking to interdict their advancing foes well before they reached their objective.

Proper training and leadership might have gone far in raising standards of discipline and combat effectiveness; but many Argentines suffered from the absence of either or both, so that once pitted against units almost invariably

Argentine infantry. The junta committed a fundamental error in not deploying its best troops for the defence of the Falklands – even when the Argentine High Command was well aware of the high standard of forces the British dispatched to reclaim the islands. Even while deployed in entrenched positions and benefiting from superior firepower, the Argentines stood little chance of repelling an offensive waged by largely elite forces. (Imperial War Museum, FKD 303)

their superior in these respects, they stood little chance of success. There is no suggestion here that Argentine forces offered only token resistance; only that when faced by troops clearly their superior in all respects apart from firepower and numbers, the odds stood decidedly in favour of those whose high standards of leadership, training, discipline, motivation and morale stood second to none in the world. It happened that the already-impressive 3 Commando Brigade stood on seven-day standby in the UK and thus was most likely first to deploy; but the judicious decision to send several other elite units (and their support elements) – quite apart from the SAS and SBS, which played important roles in gathering intelligence in the course of patrolling and in 'hides' across both the islands – fundamentally contributed to success in a remarkably short period.

By remaining in static positions and failing to patrol aggressively, the Argentines condemned themselves to operational blindness thus enabling the British to move undetected over a wide area on a strategic scale, as well as at the tactical level – approaching many defensive positions with little or no detection, thereby injecting the element of surprise into their existing practice of pursuing the doctrine of 'deliberate attack'. Failure to gather – much less assess – intelligence left, for instance, the defenders at Goose Green completely ignorant of 2 Para's approach, and also caused them to overestimate the strength of that unit once the assault began – largely owing to the panic arising out of the defenders' surprise at its sudden appearance and leaving them demoralized and unwilling to fight with the tenacity required to repel 2 Para's determined, yet poorly coordinated attack. Conversely, regular patrolling enabled the British to collect vital intelligence about Argentine defensive positions prior to their assaults of 11–14 June – a clear improvement on the bitter lesson learned at Goose Green where neither the defenders' dispositions nor numbers were accurately known.

THE BATTLEFIELDS TODAY

Stanley contains a number of sites connected with the conflict, including the Town Hall, scene of Governor Rex Hunt's capitulation, while along Ross Road outside the Upland Goose Hotel may be found the route taken by various Argentine tracked personnel carriers on the day of invasion. Passing down Reservoir Road near the King Edward Memorial Hospital one can trace part of the route taken by members of NP 8901 after their surrender. Government House, with its distinctive conservatory and extended lawn, remains largely as it appeared in 1982, albeit partly modernized and with the addition of a Deputy Governor's residence beside it. The present Governor's office remains almost identical in appearance to that occupied for ten weeks by Menéndez, with most of the original furniture retained. The Liberation Monument in Stanley lists the names of all British personnel killed in the conflict.

At Grytviken, South Georgia, a commemorative plague mounted on stone stands beside the flagpole on which M Coy, 42 Commando, raised its flag to signify the retaking of the island. The old whaling station remains, as does the old generator station at Leith, over which the Argentines raised their flag on the day they landed.

Government House, Stanley. Apart from the addition of the Deputy Governor's residence in 2002, which partially blocks the view of the main building from Ross Road, the main structure has remained virtually unchanged since 1982, including the furniture in the Governor's office. (Imagery provided by RAF Photographic Section, MPC/© UK MoD Crown Copyright 2011)

The grass airstrip at Pebble Island remains, but the wreckage of the Pucarás and other aircraft has long since been cleared away, apart from the remains of a burnt-out Skyvan PA-50.

Owing to its extreme isolation and the absence of much development on the islands, the six main battlefields remain largely untouched, as in the case of Goose Green, or entirely untouched, as may be discovered upon visiting the sites of the five engagements fought amongst the rocky features immediately west of Stanley. Those intrepid enough to visit the Falklands in the first instance will require more than merely the considerable patience to reach them, but a good deal of stamina once there. Visitors will find the following indispensable: a Land Rover, stout boots, warm and waterproof clothing, and a good pair of lungs as any proper investigation of the battlefields demands a substantial amount of walking, particularly over rough, often wet and slippery, elevated ground. Bear in mind that nearly all the detritus of war has been cleared from the islands, some of it systematically by Explosive Ordnance Disposal (EOD) personnel, the remainder by souvenir-seeking tourists or the islanders themselves. Nonetheless, some features remain, including Argentine dugouts still recognizable amidst the rocky landscape.

At Goose Green the gorse gully where Lt. Col. Jones was killed remains, though the trench from which the fatal bullet was fired, though still visible, has been filled in. A memorial obelisk stands on the spot where 'H' fell. Boca House has since been demolished, but its foundations are still to be seen. Visitors should be aware that minefields remain on the Goose Green battlefield. From 2 Para's Start Line at the northern end of Burnside Pond and Camilla Creek, it is about a 2-mile (3km) walk to the position of the main Argentine defences, with Darwin to the left and the remains of Boca House on the right. The airfield is about another mile further south and the actual Goose Green settlement another half a mile to the south-west.

At the base of the western end of Mt Longdon are two fenced-off minefields into which the lead sections of B Coy, 3 Para, strayed, thereby alerting the Argentine defenders. Other uncleared minefields remain in the vicinity. A large memorial cross stands near the crest of Longdon's north-facing slope and a stone memorial of 3 Para's fallen stands on 'Fly Half', which rises to an elevation of about 500ft (150m), as does 'Full Back'. As tributes to the fallen, friends and family have placed on the sites of their respective loved one's deaths brass plaques mounted on flat stones. A wooden cross marks the site of the Milan crew's deaths. A large number of Argentine bunkers remain, though time and the elements have collapsed most of their roofs of turf, logs and tin. Several

105mm recoilless rifles still stand amongst the Argentine defensive positions. From the summit of Longdon, looking south, one can see Tumbledown about 1¹/₂ miles (2km) away.

A rock monument stands on the summit of Mt Harriet, a climb of about 800ft (240m). An Argentine mortar, completely rusted, remains upright on the western slope. A large white cross stands on a ridge overlooking the Fitzroy–Stanley road. From there, looking north, one can see, weather permitting of course, Two Sisters about 1¹/₂ miles (2km) away, with the highest point reaching over 1,000ft (300m) from its base. Goat Ridge, behind which lie mortar bomb casings, stands about midway between Two Sisters and Mt Harriet – with 1¹/₂ miles (2km) measured between their respective summits. At least one Argentine dugout remains easily discernible on Mt Tumbledown, and as well as the various memorial plaques on its summit can be seen an impressive cross at whose base a brass plaque bears the names of the Scots Guardsmen who were killed in that action. Reaching Tumbledown's summit requires a climb of more than 600ft (180m). A 105mm recoilless rifle still stands on the western end of Wireless Ridge, at an elevation of approximately 250ft (75m) and from which one can see the summit of Mt Longdon about 2 miles (3km) to the west and that of Tumbledown about 1¹/₂ miles (2km) to the south. At Fitzroy stands a large white cross at the Welsh Guards memorial, together with a stone cairn surrounded by a white picket fence. Another memorial to the battalion in the form of a large Celtic cross bearing the names of the 32 Guardsmen who died on *Sir Galahad* stands at the headland.

Apart from a handful of British service personnel whose families have specifically requested that they remain *in situ*, most of the fallen from the conflict were sent home and lie in churchyards and military cemeteries across the UK. However, Blue Beach Cemetery in Stanley, which overlooks the Argentine landing site, contains the graves of 14 British personnel. As Argentina refused to accept the repatriation of its dead on the basis that the islands are regarded as home soil, 237 Argentine personnel remain interred in the military cemetery at Darwin.

LEFT
The Royal Marines' Falklands Memorial at Southsea, Hampshire, outside the RM Barracks. This depicts a Marine during the 'yomp' – a long-distance march carrying full kit – across East Falkland. Yomp is RM slang for 'Your own marching pace'. (Bridgeman Art Library, EDF 291123)

RIGHT
Argentine cemetery at Darwin. The British government offered to repatriate the bodies of Argentine dead, but the authorities in Buenos Aires refused on the grounds that the Falklands already constituted home soil. Consequently, six months after the war the bodies were disinterred from their various makeshift graves and reburied here. (Imperial War Museum, FKD 2542)

BIBLIOGRAPHY AND FURTHER READING

Adkin, Mark, *Goose Green: A Battle is Fought to be Won*, Phoenix (2000)

Anderson, Duncan, *The Falklands War 1982*, Osprey Publishing (2002)

Bicheno, Hugh, *Razor's Edge: The Unofficial History of the Falklands War*, Phoenix (2007)

Bishop, Patrick and Witherow, John, *Winter War: The Falklands Conflict*, Quartet Books (1982)

Briasco, Jesus Romero and Huertas, Salvador Mafe, *Falklands: Witness of Battles*, Frederico Domenech (1985)

Burns, Jimmy, *The Land that Lost its Heroes: How Argentina Lost the Falklands War*, Bloomsbury Publishing (2002)

Clapp, Michael and Southby-Tailyour, Ewen, *Amphibious Assault Falklands: The Battle of San Carlos Water*, Pen & Sword Maritime (2007)

Cooksey, Jon, *Special Air Service: Pebble Island – The Falklands War 1982*, Pen & Sword Military (2007)

——, *3 Para: Mount Longdon – The Bloodiest Battle*, Leo Cooper (2004)

Fitz-Gibbon, Spencer, *Not Mentioned in Dispatches: The History and Mythology of the Battle of Goose Green*, Lutterworth Press (2001)

Fowler, William, *Battle for the Falklands (1): Land Forces*, Osprey Publishing (2002)

Freedman, Lawrence, *The Official History of the Falklands Campaign. Vol. I: The Origins of the Falklands War*, Routledge (2007)

——, *The Official History of the Falklands Campaign. Vol. II: War and Diplomacy*, Routledge (2007)

Frost, Major-General John, *2 Para in the Falklands: The Battalion at War*, Buchan & Enright (1983)

Hastings, Max and Jenkins, Simon, *Battle for the Falklands*, Pan (2010)

Jennings, Christian and Adrian Weale, *Green-Eyed Boys: 3 Para and the Battle for Mount Longdon*, HarperCollins (1996)

Middlebrook, Martin, *Argentine Fight for the Falklands*, Pen & Sword Military (2009)

——, *The Falklands War 1982*, Penguin Classics (2007)

Oakley, Derek, *The Falklands Military Machine*, The History Press (2002)

Orgill, Andrew, *The Falklands War: Background, Conflict, Aftermath*, Mansell (1993)

Ramsey, Gordon, *The Falklands Then and Now*, After the Battle (2009)

Southby-Tailyour, Ewen, *Reasons in Writing: A Commando's View of the Falklands War*, Leo Cooper (2003)

Thompson, Julian, *3 Commando Brigade in the Falklands: No Picnic*, Pen & Sword Military (2008)

Van Der Bijl, Nick and Aldea, David, *5th Infantry Brigade in the Falklands*, Pen & Sword (2002)

Van Der Bijl, Nick, *Argentine Forces in the Falklands*, Osprey Publishing (2005)

——, *Nine Battles to Stanley*, Leo Cooper (1999)

——, *Victory in the Falklands*, Pen & Sword Military (2007)

Vaux, Nick, *March to the South Atlantic: 42 Commando Royal Marines in the Falklands War*, Buchan & Enright (1986)

——, *Take That Hill: Royal Marines in the Falklands War*, Brassey's (1987)

Wilsey, John, *H Jones VC: The Life and Death of an Unusual Hero*, Hutchinson (2000)

Woodward, Sandy, with Patrick Robinson, *One Hundred Days: The Memoirs of the Falklands Battle Group Commander*, HarperCollins (2010)

INDEX

References to illustrations are shown in **bold**.